Diabetic Diet

Cookbook for Beginners UK

1600 Days Easy, Nutritious and Delicious Diabetes Recipes for Managing Diabetes and Regaining Vitality and Energy Incl. 21-Day Meal Plan

Scarlett Hilton

CONTENTS

Introduction

As a person living with diabetes, I understand the challenges that come with managing the condition. It can be overwhelming to navigate the world of food and nutrition, especially for those who are newly diagnosed. That's why I decided to write the Diabetic Diet Cookbook for Beginners: 1600 Days Easy, Nutritious and Delicious Diabetes Recipes for Managing Diabetes and Regaining Vitality and Energy Incl. 21-Day Meal Plan. This cookbook is designed to help individuals with diabetes take control of their health and enjoy delicious, nutritious meals.

I have been living with diabetes for over a decade, and I have learned a lot about managing the condition through food and lifestyle. I have also worked with many individuals with diabetes as a registered dietitian and nutritionist. Over the years, I have developed a passion for creating healthy and delicious meals that are tailored to the needs of individuals with diabetes. I decided to compile my knowledge and experience into this cookbook to help others who are struggling with the condition.

There are many cookbooks and resources available for individuals with diabetes, but I noticed a gap in the market for a cookbook that is tailored to beginners. Many individuals who are newly diagnosed with diabetes feel overwhelmed and unsure of where to start when it comes to nutrition. This cookbook is designed to provide a step-by-step guide to managing diabetes through food, with easy and delicious recipes that anyone can make.

The Diabetic Diet Cookbook for Beginners: 1600 Days Easy, Nutritious and Delicious Diabetes Recipes for Managing Diabetes and Regaining Vitality and Energy Incl. 21-Day Meal Plan is a comprehensive guide to managing diabetes through food. It is designed for beginners who are looking for an easy and enjoyable way to take control of their health. This cookbook is packed with benefits, including a variety of easy and delicious recipes, clear nutritional information, and tips and tricks for managing diabetes through food and lifestyle. I hope that this cookbook will bring a range of benefits to readers and help them to enjoy a healthy and fulfilling life with diabetes.

What are the symptoms of Diabetes?

Diabetes is a chronic condition that affects how the body processes blood sugar (glucose). It occurs when the body either does not produce enough insulin or cannot use the insulin it produces effectively. Insulin is a hormone that helps regulate blood sugar levels, and without it, blood sugar can build up in the bloodstream and lead to various health problems. Here are some of the most common symptoms of diabetes:

● **Increased thirst**

Feeling thirsty more often than usual can be a sign of diabetes. This is because high blood sugar levels can cause the body to lose more fluid, leading to dehydration.

● **Frequent urination**

People with diabetes may need to urinate more often than usual, particularly at night. This is because high blood sugar levels can cause the kidneys to work harder to filter out excess glucose.

● **Fatigue**

Feeling tired or run down is a common symptom of diabetes, as the body may not be able to use glucose effectively for energy.

● **Blurred vision**

High blood sugar levels can cause changes in the lenses of the eyes, leading to blurred vision.

● **Slow healing**

People with diabetes may experience slow healing of wounds and infections due to high blood sugar levels, which can impair the immune system.

● **Numbness or tingling**

Diabetes can cause nerve damage over time, leading to numbness or tingling in the hands and feet.

● **Unexplained weight loss**

People with diabetes may experience unexplained weight loss, even if they are eating more than usual. This is because the body may be breaking down fat and muscle tissue for energy instead of using glucose.

It's important to note that not everyone with diabetes will experience all of these symptoms, and some people may not experience any symptoms at all. In some cases, diabetes may be diagnosed during routine blood tests. If you are experiencing any of these symptoms, it's important to see a healthcare provider for testing and diagnosis. Early diagnosis and treatment of diabetes can help prevent complications and improve outcomes.

What are the different types of Diabetes?

There are several types of diabetes, each with their own causes, symptoms, and treatment approaches. Here are the most common types of diabetes:

● **Type 1 diabetes**

Type 1 diabetes, also known as juvenile diabetes, is an autoimmune disease in which the body's immune system mistakenly attacks and destroys the cells in the pancreas that produce insulin. As a result, people with type 1 diabetes do not produce enough insulin and must take insulin injections or use an insulin pump to manage their blood sugar levels. Type 1 diabetes usually develops in childhood or adolescence but can occur at any age.

- **Type 2 diabetes**

Type 2 diabetes is the most common type of diabetes, accounting for around 90% of cases. It occurs when the body becomes resistant to insulin or does not produce enough insulin to meet its needs. Type 2 diabetes is often associated with lifestyle factors such as obesity, lack of physical activity, and poor diet. It can be managed through lifestyle changes, medication, and insulin therapy if necessary.

- **Gestational diabetes**

Gestational diabetes occurs during pregnancy and usually resolves after delivery. It can occur when the body becomes less sensitive to insulin during pregnancy, leading to high blood sugar levels. Gestational diabetes can increase the risk of complications during pregnancy and delivery and can also increase the risk of developing type 2 diabetes later in life.

- **Pre-diabetes**

Pre-diabetes occurs when blood sugar levels are higher than normal but not high enough to be diagnosed as type 2 diabetes. Pre-diabetes can increase the risk of developing type 2 diabetes if lifestyle changes are not made.

- **Monogenic diabetes**

Monogenic diabetes is a rare form of diabetes caused by genetic mutations. It can be inherited from one or both parents and often affects young adults or children. Treatment for monogenic diabetes may differ from other types of diabetes and may involve oral medication instead of insulin injections.

- **Secondary diabetes**

Secondary diabetes occurs as a result of another medical condition or medication, such as pancreatitis, cystic fibrosis, or steroid use. Treatment involves managing the underlying condition or adjusting medication as necessary.

It's important to note that the symptoms and treatment approaches for each type of diabetes can vary, and it's important to work with a healthcare provider to make an accurate diagnosis and develop an individualized treatment plan.

How can diet help manage Diabetes?

Diet plays a crucial role in managing diabetes. A healthy and balanced diet can help control blood sugar levels, reduce the risk of complications, and improve overall health. Here are some ways in which diet can help manage diabetes:

- **Balancing carbohydrates**

Carbohydrates are the primary source of glucose in the body, and managing carbohydrate intake is a key aspect of managing diabetes. Eating consistent amounts of carbohydrates at each meal can help manage blood sugar levels and reduce the risk of highs and lows. Choosing complex carbohydrates that are high in fiber, such as whole grains, fruits, vegetables, and legumes, can help slow down the absorption of glucose into the bloodstream and prevent spikes in blood sugar levels.

- **Choosing fiber-rich foods**

Fiber can help slow down the absorption of glucose in the bloodstream, reducing the risk of spikes in blood sugar levels. Choosing foods that are high in fiber, such as fruits, vegetables, whole grains, and legumes, can help manage diabetes. Aim to include at least 25-30 grams of fiber in your diet each day.

● **Limiting unhealthy fats**

Eating too much unhealthy fat, such as saturated and trans fats, can increase the risk of heart disease and other complications associated with diabetes. Choosing healthy fats, such as monounsaturated and polyunsaturated fats, can help manage diabetes and reduce the risk of complications. Good sources of healthy fats include avocados, nuts, seeds, and fatty fish.

● **Eating lean protein**

Eating lean protein, such as chicken, fish, tofu, and legumes, can help manage blood sugar levels and promote fullness. It's important to choose protein sources that are low in saturated fat and sodium. Aim for 2-3 servings of protein each day.

● **Managing portion sizes**

Eating too much food, even if it's healthy, can lead to spikes in blood sugar levels. Managing portion sizes can help manage blood sugar levels and promote a healthy weight. Use measuring cups, a food scale, or other portion control tools to help manage portion sizes.

● **Limiting added sugars**

Eating foods that are high in added sugars, such as soda, candy, and baked goods, can cause spikes in blood sugar levels and increase the risk of complications associated with diabetes. Limiting added sugars in the diet can help manage diabetes and improve overall health. Choose naturally sweet foods such as fruit instead of foods that are high in added sugars.

● **Eating regularly**

Eating regular meals and snacks can help manage blood sugar levels and prevent highs and lows. Aim to eat three meals and one to two snacks each day, and try to eat at consistent times each day.

How to get started with a Diabetic Diet?

Getting started with a diabetic diet can seem overwhelming, but taking small steps can help make the transition easier. Here are some tips for getting started with a diabetic diet:

● **Learn about the basics of a diabetic diet**

A diabetic diet typically focuses on whole foods, lean proteins, healthy fats, and complex carbohydrates. It also limits added sugars, unhealthy fats, and processed foods. Learning about the basics of a diabetic diet can help you make informed choices when planning meals.

● **Start small**

Making too many changes at once can be overwhelming. Start by making small changes to your diet, such as swapping sugary drinks for water or choosing whole grain bread instead of white bread.

● **Plan meals ahead of time**

Planning meals ahead of time can help ensure that you have healthy options available and can prevent impulse choices that may not align with your dietary goals. Consider meal prepping for the week ahead or making a grocery list to help you stay on track.

- **Experiment with new recipes**

Trying new recipes can help keep mealtime interesting and prevent boredom with the same old meals. Look for diabetes-friendly recipes that are easy to follow and use whole, nutrient-dense ingredients.

- **Monitor your blood sugar levels**

As you make changes to your diet, it's important to monitor your blood sugar levels to see how your body responds. This can help you determine what foods and meal patterns work best for you.

- **Seek support**

Managing diabetes can be challenging, and it's important to seek support from friends, family, or a healthcare professional. Consider joining a diabetes support group or working with a registered dietitian for personalized guidance and support.

Getting started with a diabetic diet involves making small, manageable changes to your diet and seeking guidance from healthcare professionals as needed. With time and practice, a diabetic diet can become a healthy and enjoyable way of eating that helps manage blood sugar levels and promotes overall health.

Breakfast Recipes

Open-faced Poached Egg Sandwiches

Servings:4
Cooking Time:8minutes
Ingredients:

- 2 ounces goat cheese, crumbled and softened (½ cup)
- ½ teaspoon lemon juice
- ⅛ teaspoon pepper
- 2 whole-wheat English muffins, split in half, toasted, and still warm
- 1 small tomato, cored, seeded, and sliced thin (about 8 slices)
- 2 teaspoons extra-virgin olive oil
- 1 shallot, minced
- 1 garlic clove, minced
- 4 ounces (4 cups) baby spinach
- ⅛ teaspoon salt
- 2 tablespoons distilled vinegar
- 4 large eggs

Directions:

1. Adjust oven rack to middle position and heat oven to 300 degrees. Stir goat cheese, lemon juice, and pepper together in bowl until smooth. Spread goat cheese mixture evenly over warm English muffin halves and top with tomato slices. Arrange English muffins on rimmed baking sheet and keep warm in oven while preparing spinach and eggs.
2. Heat oil in 12-inch nonstick skillet over medium heat until shimmering. Add shallot and cook until softened, about 2 minutes. Stir in garlic and cook until fragrant, about 30 seconds. Stir in spinach and salt and cook until wilted, about 1 minute. Using tongs, squeeze out any excess moisture from spinach, then divide evenly among English muffins.
3. Wipe skillet clean with paper towels, then fill it nearly to rim with water. Add vinegar and bring to boil over high heat. Meanwhile, crack eggs into two teacups (2 eggs in each). Reduce water to simmer. Gently tip cups so eggs slide into skillet simultaneously. Remove skillet from heat, cover, and poach eggs for 4 minutes (add 30 seconds for firm yolks).
4. Using slotted spoon, gently lift eggs from water and let drain before laying them on top of spinach. Serve immediately.

Nutrition Info:

- Info210 cal., 11g fat (4g sag. fat), 195mg chol, 350mg sod., 17g carb (4g sugars, 3g fiber), 13g pro.

Blackberry Smoothies

Servings:4
Cooking Time: 10 Minutes
Ingredients:

- 1 cup orange juice
- 1 cup (8 ounces) plain yogurt
- 2 to 3 tablespoons honey
- 1 1/2 cups fresh or frozen blackberries
- 1/2 cup frozen unsweetened mixed berries
- Additional blackberries and yogurt, optional

Directions:

1. In a blender, combine the first five ingredients; cover and process for about 15 seconds or until smooth. Pour into chilled glasses; serve immediately. If desired top with additional blackberries and yogurt.

Nutrition Info:

- Info130 cal., 2g fat (1g sat. fat), 8mg chol., 29mg sod., 26g carb. (21g sugars, 3g fiber), 3g pro.

Breakfast Grilled Swiss Cheese And Rye

Servings: 2
Cooking Time:7 Minutes
Ingredients:

- 2 slices rye bread
- 4 teaspoons reduced-fat margarine (35% vegetable oil)
- 2 large eggs
- 1 1/2 ounces sliced, reduced-fat Swiss cheese, torn in small pieces

Directions:

1. Spread one side of each bread slice with 1 teaspoon margarine and set aside.
2. Place a medium skillet over medium heat until hot. Coat with nonstick cooking spray and add the egg substitute. Cook 1 minute without stirring. Using a rubber spatula, lift up the edges to allow the uncooked portion to run under. Cook 1–2 minutes longer or until eggs are almost set and beginning to puff up slightly. Flip and cook 30 seconds.
3. Remove the skillet from the heat and spoon half of the eggs on the unbuttered sides of two of the bread slices. Arrange equal amounts of the cheese evenly over each piece.
4. Return the skillet to medium heat until hot. Coat the skillet with nonstick cooking spray. Add the two sandwiches and cook 3 minutes. If the cheese doesn't melt when frying the sandwich bottom, put it under the broiler until brown. Using a serrated knife, cut each sandwich in half.

Nutrition Info:

- Info250 cal., 13g fat (4g sag. fat), 200mg chol, 360mg sod., 17g carb (2g sugars, 2g fiber), 16g pro.

Stuffed Mushrooms

Servings:6
Cooking Time:18 Minutes
Ingredients:

- 24 large white mushrooms (1¾ to 2 inches in diameter), stems removed and reserved
- 2 tablespoons extra-virgin olive oil
- ¼ teaspoon salt
- ¼ teaspoon pepper
- 1 small shallot, minced
- 2 garlic cloves, minced
- ¼ cup dry white wine
- 1 ounce Parmesan cheese, grated (½ cup)
- 1 teaspoon minced fresh thyme
- 1 teaspoon lemon juice
- 1 tablespoon minced fresh parsley

Directions:

1. Adjust oven rack to middle position and heat oven to 425 degrees. Line rimmed baking sheet with aluminum foil. Toss mushroom caps with 1 tablespoon oil, salt, and ⅛ teaspoon pepper and arrange gill side up on prepared sheet. Bake until mushrooms release their moisture and shrink in size, about 15 minutes. Flip caps and continue to bake until well browned, about 5 minutes; set aside.
2. Meanwhile, pulse reserved mushroom stems, shallot, garlic, and ⅛ teaspoon pepper in food processor until finely chopped, 10 to 14 pulses. Heat remaining 1 tablespoon oil in 8-inch nonstick skillet over medium heat until shimmering. Add stem mixture and cook until dry and golden brown, about 5 minutes. Stir in wine and cook until evaporated and mixture thickens, about 2 minutes. Transfer to bowl and let cool slightly. Stir in 6 tablespoons Parmesan, thyme, and lemon juice.
3. Flip caps gill side up. Divide stuffing evenly among caps and top with remaining 2 tablespoons Parmesan. Bake until stuffing is heated through and Parmesan is golden brown, about 15 minutes. Transfer to serving platter and sprinkle with parsley. Serve.

Nutrition Info:

- Info90 cal., 6g fat (1g sag. fat), 5mg chol, 190mg sod., 3g carb (2g sugars, 0g fiber), 3g pro.

Yogurt Parfaits

Servings:4
Cooking Time:8 Minutes
Ingredients:

- 1 cup whole almonds, toasted and chopped
- ½ cup raw sunflower seeds, toasted
- 3 cups low-fat plain yogurt
- 20 ounces (4 cups) blackberries, blueberries, raspberries, and/or sliced strawberries

Directions:
1. Combine almonds and sunflower seeds in bowl. Using four 16-ounce glasses, spoon ¼ cup yogurt into each glass, then top with ⅓ cup berries, followed by 2 tablespoons nut mixture. Repeat layering process 2 more times with remaining yogurt, berries, and nut mixture. Serve.

Nutrition Info:
- Info480 cal., 29g fat (4g sag. fat), 10mg chol, 130mg sod., 39g carb (24g sugars, 11g fiber), 22g pro.

Roasted Vegetable Strata

Servings:8
Cooking Time: 40 Minutes
Ingredients:

- 3 large zucchini, halved lengthwise and cut into 3/4-inch slices
- 1 each medium red, yellow and orange peppers, cut into 1-inch pieces
- 2 tablespoons olive oil
- 1 teaspoon dried oregano
- 1/2 teaspoon salt
- 1/2 teaspoon pepper
- 1/2 teaspoon dried basil
- 1 medium tomato, chopped
- 1 loaf (1 pound) unsliced crusty Italian bread
- 1/2 cup shredded sharp cheddar cheese
- 1/2 cup shredded Asiago cheese
- 6 large eggs
- 2 cups fat-free milk

Directions:
1. Preheat oven to 400°. Toss zucchini and peppers with oil and seasonings; transfer to a 15x10x1-in. pan. Roast until tender, 25-30 minutes, stirring once. Stir in tomato; cool slightly.
2. Trim ends from bread; cut into 1-in. slices. In a greased 13x9-in. baking dish, layer half of each of the following: bread, roasted vegetables and cheeses. Repeat layers. Whisk together eggs and milk; pour evenly over top. Refrigerate, covered, 6 hours or overnight.
3. Preheat oven to 375°. Remove casserole from refrigerator while oven heats. Bake, uncovered, until golden brown, 40-50 minutes. Let stand 5-10 minutes before cutting.

Nutrition Info:
- Info349 cal., 14g fat (5g sat. fat), 154mg chol., 642mg sod., 40g carb. (9g sugars, 4g fiber), 17g pro.

English Muffin Melts

Servings: 8
Cooking Time:3 Minutes
Ingredients:

- 4 whole-wheat English muffins, cut in half
- 2 tablespoons reduced-fat mayonnaise
- 3 ounces sliced reduced-fat Swiss cheese, torn in small pieces
- 4 ounces oven-roasted deli turkey, finely chopped

Directions:
1. Preheat the broiler.
2. Arrange the muffin halves on a baking sheet and place under the broiler for 1–2 minutes or until lightly toasted. Remove from broiler and spread 3/4 teaspoon mayonnaise over each muffin half.
3. Arrange the cheese pieces evenly on each muffin half and top with the turkey.
4. Return to the broiler and cook 3 minutes, or until the turkey is just beginning to turn golden and the cheese has melted.

Nutrition Info:
- Info120 cal., 3g fat (1g sag. fat), 15mg chol, 290mg sod., 15g carb (3g sugars, 2g fiber), 9g pro.

Steel-cut Oatmeal With Blueberries And Almonds

Servings:4
Cooking Time: 12 Hours
Ingredients:

- 3 cups water
- 1 cup steel-cut oats
- ¼ teaspoon salt
- ½ cup 1 percent low-fat milk
- 1 tablespoon packed brown sugar
- ¼ teaspoon ground cinnamon
- Pinch ground nutmeg
- 2½ ounces (½ cup) blueberries
- ⅓ cup whole almonds, toasted and chopped coarse

Directions:
1. Bring water to boil in large saucepan over high heat. Off heat, stir in oats and salt, cover, and let sit for at least 12 hours or up to 24 hours.
2. Stir milk, sugar, cinnamon, and nutmeg into oats and bring to boil over medium-high heat. Reduce heat to medium and cook, stirring occasionally, until oats are softened but still retain some chew and mixture thickens and resembles warm pudding, 4 to 6 minutes.
3. Remove saucepan from heat and let sit for 5 minutes. Stir to recombine and serve, sprinkling individual portions with blueberries and almonds.

Nutrition Info:

- Info270 cal., 8g fat (1g sag. fat), 0mg chol, 170mg sod., 42g carb (8g sugars, 6g fiber), 9g pro.

Ginger-kale Smoothies

Servings:2
Cooking Time: 15 Minutes
Ingredients:

- 1 1/4 cups orange juice
- 1 teaspoon lemon juice
- 2 cups torn fresh kale
- 1 medium apple, peeled and coarsely chopped
- 1 tablespoon minced fresh gingerroot
- 4 ice cubes
- 1/8 teaspoon ground cinnamon
- 1/8 teaspoon ground turmeric or 1/4-inch piece fresh turmeric, peeled and finely chopped
- Dash cayenne pepper

Directions:
1. Place all ingredients in a blender; cover and process until blended. Serve the smoothie immediately.

Nutrition Info:

- Info121 cal., 0 fat (0 sat. fat), 0 chol., 22mg sod., 29g carb. (21g sugars, 2g fiber), 1g pro.

Apple Spiced Tea

Servings:1
Cooking Time: 10 Minutes
Ingredients:

- 1/2 cup apple cider or juice
- 1/4 teaspoon minced fresh gingerroot
- 2 whole allspice
- 2 whole cloves
- 1 black tea bag
- 1/2 cup boiling water
- 1 tablespoon brown sugar

Directions:
1. In a small bowl, combine the first five ingredients. Add boiling water. Cover and steep for 5 minutes. Strain, discarding tea bag and spices. Stir in sugar. Serve immediately.

Nutrition Info:

- Info112 cal., 0 fat (0 sat. fat), 0 chol., 12mg sod., 28g carb. (27g sugars, 0 fiber), 0 pro.

Peach Cranberry Quick Bread

Servings: 14
Cooking Time:45 Minutes
Ingredients:

- 1 (15.6-ounce) box cranberry quick bread and muffin mix
- 1 cup water
- 1/2 cup egg substitute or 4 large egg whites
- 2 tablespoons canola oil
- 2 cups chopped frozen and thawed unsweetened peaches

Directions:

1. Preheat the oven to 375°F.
2. Coat a nonstick 9 × 5-inch loaf pan with nonstick cooking spray.
3. Beat the bread mix, water, egg substitute, and oil in a medium bowl for 50 strokes or until well blended. Stir in the peaches and spoon into the loaf pan. Bake 45 minutes or until a wooden toothpick comes out clean.
4. Place the loaf pan on a wire rack for 20 minutes before removing the bread from the pan. Cool completely for peak flavor and texture.

Nutrition Info:

- Info150 cal., 3g fat (0g sag. fat), 0mg chol, 150mg sod., 29g carb (15g sugars, 1g fiber), 3g pro.

Frittata With Spinach, Bell Pepper, And Basil

Servings:4
Cooking Time:30minutes
Ingredients:

- 8 large eggs
- 1 ounce Parmesan cheese, grated (½ cup)
- 3 tablespoons 1 percent low-fat milk
- 2 tablespoons chopped fresh basil
- ⅛ teaspoon salt
- ¼ teaspoon pepper
- 2 teaspoons extra-virgin olive oil
- 1 small onion, chopped fine
- 1 red bell pepper, stemmed, seeded, and cut into 2-inch matchsticks
- 1 garlic clove, minced
- 3 ounces (3 cups) baby spinach

Directions:

1. Adjust oven rack to middle position and heat oven to 350 degrees. Beat eggs, Parmesan, milk, basil, salt, and pepper with fork in bowl until eggs are thoroughly combined and color is pure yellow; do not overbeat.
2. Heat oil in 10-inch ovensafe nonstick skillet over medium heat until shimmering. Add onion and bell pepper and cook until softened, about 5 minutes. Stir in garlic and cook until fragrant, about 30 seconds. Stir in spinach and cook until wilted, about 1 minute.
3. Add egg mixture and, using rubber spatula, constantly and firmly scrape along bottom and sides of skillet until eggs begin to clump and spatula just leaves trail on bottom of pan but eggs are still very wet, about 30 seconds. Smooth curds into even layer and cook, without stirring, for 30 seconds.
4. Transfer skillet to oven and bake until frittata is slightly puffy and surface is dry and bounces back when lightly pressed, 6 to 9 minutes. Run spatula around edge of skillet to loosen frittata, then carefully slide it out onto serving plate. Let sit for 5 minutes before slicing and serving.

Nutrition Info:

- Info230 cal., 14g fat (4g sag. fat), 380mg chol, 370mg sod., 7g carb (3g sugars, 2g fiber), 17g pro.

Cheesy Mushroom Omelet

Servings: 2
Cooking Time:6 Minutes
Ingredients:
- 6 ounces sliced mushrooms
- 1/8 teaspoon black pepper
- 1/3 cup finely chopped green onion (green and white parts)
- 1 cup egg substitute
- 2 tablespoons crumbled bleu cheese (about 1/4 cup) or 1/4 cup shredded, reduced-fat, sharp cheddar cheese

Directions:
1. Place a small skillet over medium-high heat until hot. Coat with nonstick cooking spray and add mushrooms and pepper. Coat the mushrooms with nonstick cooking spray and cook 4 minutes or until soft, stirring frequently.
2. Add the onions and cook 1 minute longer. Set the pan aside.
3. Place another small skillet over medium heat until hot. Coat with nonstick cooking spray and add the egg substitute. Cook 1 minute without stirring. Using a rubber spatula, lift up the edges to allow the uncooked portion to run under. Cook 1–2 minutes longer or until eggs are almost set and beginning to puff up slightly.
4. Spoon the mushroom mixture on one half of the omelet, sprinkle the cheese evenly over the mushrooms, and gently fold over. Cut in half to serve.

Nutrition Info:
- Info110 cal., 2g fat (1g sag. fat), 5mg chol, 340mg sod., 6g carb (3g sugars, 1g fiber), 16g pro.

Fried Eggs With Sweet Potatoes And Turkey Sausage

Servings:6
Cooking Time:20minutes
Ingredients:
- 1½ pounds sweet potatoes, peeled and cut into ¼-inch pieces
- 2 tablespoons extra-virgin olive oil
- ¼ teaspoon pepper
- 8 ounces sweet Italian turkey sausage, casings removed
- 1 onion, chopped fine
- 2 garlic cloves, minced
- 1 teaspoon minced fresh thyme
- 1 teaspoon minced fresh sage
- ¼ teaspoon grated lemon zest, plus lemon wedges for serving
- Pinch red pepper flakes
- 6 large eggs
- 2 tablespoons minced fresh parsley

Directions:
1. Microwave potatoes, 1 teaspoon oil, and pepper in covered bowl, stirring occasionally, until potatoes begin to soften, 6 to 8 minutes. Drain potatoes well and return to bowl.
2. Heat 1 teaspoon oil in 12-inch nonstick skillet over medium-high heat until shimmering. Add sausage and onion and cook, breaking up sausage with wooden spoon, until sausage is lightly browned and onion is softened, 5 to 7 minutes. Stir in garlic, thyme, sage, lemon zest, and pepper flakes and cook until fragrant, about 30 seconds. Transfer sausage mixture to separate bowl.
3. Wipe skillet clean with paper towel. Heat 1 tablespoon oil in now-empty skillet over medium heat until shimmering. Add potatoes and cook, stirring occasionally, until tender and well browned, about 4 minutes. Stir in sausage mixture and cook until heated through, about 2 minutes. Transfer to serving platter and tent with aluminum foil.
4. Wipe skillet clean with paper towel. Crack 3 eggs into bowl. Crack remaining 3 eggs into second bowl. Heat remaining 1 teaspoon oil in now-empty skillet and heat over medium-low heat until shimmering. Working quickly, pour 1 bowl of eggs into one side of pan and second bowl of eggs into other side of pan. Cover and cook for 1 minute. Remove skillet from heat and let sit, covered, 15 to 45 seconds for runny yolks (white around edge of yolk will be barely opaque), 45 to 60 seconds for soft but set yolks, and about 2 minutes for medium-set yolks. Using rubber spatula, gently transfer eggs on top of hash. Sprinkle with parsley and serve.

Nutrition Info:
- Info270 cal., 14g fat (2g sag. fat), 210mg chol, 380mg sod., 23g carb (7g sugars, 4g fiber), 15g pro.

Appetizers And Snacks Recipes

Gorgonzola Polenta Bites

Servings:16
Cooking Time: 25 Minutes
Ingredients:

- 1/3 cup balsamic vinegar
- 1 tablespoon orange marmalade
- 1/2 cup panko (Japanese) bread crumbs
- 1 tube (18 ounces) polenta, cut into 16 slices
- 2 tablespoons olive oil
- 1/2 cup crumbled Gorgonzola cheese
- 3 tablespoons dried currants, optional

Directions:

1. In a small saucepan, combine vinegar and marmalade. Bring to a boil; cook 5-7 minutes or until liquid is reduced to 2 tablespoons.
2. Meanwhile, place bread crumbs in a shallow bowl. Press both sides of the polenta slices in bread crumbs. In a large skillet, heat oil over medium-high heat. Add polenta in batches; cook for 2-4 minutes on each side or until slices are golden brown.
3. Arrange polenta on a serving platter; spoon cheese over top. If desired, sprinkle with currants; drizzle with vinegar mixture. Serve bites warm or at room temperature.

Nutrition Info:

- Info67 cal., 3g fat (1g sat. fat), 3mg chol., 161mg sod., 9g carb. (3g sugars, 0 fiber), 1g pro.

Creamy Apricot Fruit Dip

Servings: 4
Cooking Time: 5 Minutes
Ingredients:

- 1/3 cup fat-free vanilla-flavored yogurt
- 1/4 cup fat-free whipped topping
- 2 tablespoons apricot all-fruit spread
- 2 cups whole strawberries or 2 medium apples, halved, cored, and sliced

Directions:

1. In a small bowl, whisk the yogurt, whipped topping, and fruit spread until well blended.
2. Serve with fruit.

Nutrition Info:

- Info60 cal., 0g fat (0g sag. fat), 0mg chol, 15mg sod., 14g carb (9g sugars, 2g fiber), 1g pro.

Homemade Guacamole

Servings:2
Cooking Time: 10 Minutes
Ingredients:

- 3 medium ripe avocados, peeled and cubed
- 1 garlic clove, minced
- 1/4 to 1/2 teaspoon salt
- 2 medium tomatoes, seeded and chopped, optional
- 1 small onion, finely chopped
- 1/4 cup mayonnaise, optional
- 1 to 2 tablespoons lime juice
- 1 tablespoon minced fresh cilantro

Directions:

1. Mash avocados with garlic and salt. Stir in remaining ingredients.

Nutrition Info:

- Info111 calories, 10g fat (1g saturated fat), 0mg cholesterol, 43mg sodium, 6g carbohydrate (1g sugars, 5g fiber), 1g protein.

Cheesy Snack Mix

Servings:2
Cooking Time: 5 Minutes
Ingredients:
- 3 cups Corn Chex
- 3 cups Rice Chex
- 3 cups cheddar miniature pretzels
- 1/4 cup butter, melted
- 1 envelope cheesy taco seasoning
- 2 cups white cheddar popcorn

Directions:
1. In a large microwave-safe bowl, combine cereal and pretzels. In a small bowl, mix melted butter and taco seasoning; drizzle over cereal mixture and toss to coat.
2. Microwave, uncovered, on high 3-3 1/2 minutes or until heated through, stirring once every minute. Stir in popcorn. Transfer to a baking sheet to cool completely. Store snack mix in an airtight container.

Nutrition Info:
- Info151 cal., 5g fat (3g sat. fat), 11mg chol., 362mg sod., 23g carb. (2g sugars, 1g fiber), 3g pro.

Wicked Deviled Eggs

Servings:2
Cooking Time: 30 Minutes
Ingredients:
- 12 hard-cooked eggs, peeled
- 1/2 cup Miracle Whip
- 2 tablespoons cider vinegar
- 2 tablespoons prepared mustard
- 1 tablespoon minced fresh parsley or 1 teaspoon dried parsley flakes
- 1 tablespoon butter, melted
- 1 tablespoon sweet pickle relish
- 2 teaspoons Worcestershire sauce
- 1 teaspoon sweet pickle juice
- 1/2 teaspoon salt
- 1/2 teaspoon cayenne pepper
- 1/2 teaspoon pepper
- Paprika

Directions:
1. Cut eggs in half lengthwise. Remove yolks; set whites aside. In a small bowl, mash yolks. Add the Miracle Whip, vinegar, mustard, parsley, butter, relish, Worcestershire sauce, pickle juice, salt, cayenne and pepper; mix well. Stuff or pipe into egg whites.
2. Refrigerate until serving. Sprinkle with paprika.

Nutrition Info:
- Info61 cal., 5g fat (1g sat. fat), 109mg chol., 151mg sod., 1g carb. (1g sugars, 0 fiber), 3g pro.

Curried Chicken Meatball Wraps

Servings:2
Cooking Time: 20 Minutes
Ingredients:

- 1 large egg, lightly beaten
- 1 small onion, finely chopped
- 1/2 cup Rice Krispies
- 1/4 cup golden raisins
- 1/4 cup minced fresh cilantro
- 2 teaspoons curry powder
- 1/2 teaspoon salt
- 1 pound lean ground chicken
- SAUCE

- 1 cup (8 ounces) plain yogurt
- 1/4 cup minced fresh cilantro
- WRAPS
- 24 small Bibb or Boston lettuce leaves
- 1 medium carrot, shredded
- 1/2 cup golden raisins
- 1/2 cup chopped salted peanuts
- Additional minced fresh cilantro

Directions:

1. Preheat oven to 350°. In a large bowl, combine first seven ingredients. Add chicken; mix lightly but thoroughly. With wet hands, shape mixture into 24 balls (about 1 1/4-in.).
2. Place meatballs on a greased rack in a 15x10x1-in. baking pan. Bake 17-20 minutes or until cooked through.
3. In a small bowl, mix the sauce ingredients. To serve, place 1 teaspoon sauce and one meatball in each lettuce leaf; top with remaining ingredients.

Nutrition Info:

- Info72 cal., 3g fat (1g sat. fat), 22mg chol., 89mg sod., 6g carb. (4g sugars, 1g fiber), 6g pro.

Basil Spread And Water Crackers

Servings: 4
Cooking Time: 5 Minutes
Ingredients:

- 2 ounces reduced-fat garlic and herb cream cheese
- 1/2 cup finely chopped fresh basil
- 12 fat-free water crackers

Directions:

1. Stir the cream cheese and basil together in a small bowl until well blended.
2. Place 1 teaspoon spread on each cracker.

Nutrition Info:

- Info70 cal., 2g fat (1g sag. fat), 0mg chol, 200mg sod., 9g carb (1g sugars, 0g fiber), 3g pro.

Tuna Salad Stuffed Eggs

Servings: 4
Cooking Time:10 Minutes
Ingredients:

- 4 large eggs
- 1 (2.6-ounce) packet tuna (or 5-ounce can of tuna packed in water, rinsed and well drained)
- 2 tablespoons reduced-fat mayonnaise
- 1 1/2–2 tablespoons sweet pickle relish

Directions:

1. Place eggs in a medium saucepan and cover with cold water. Bring to a boil over high heat, then reduce the heat and simmer 10 minutes.
2. Meanwhile, stir the tuna, mayonnaise, and relish together in a small bowl.
3. When the eggs are cooked, remove them from the water and let stand one minute before peeling under cold running water. Cut eggs in half, lengthwise, and discard 4 egg yolk halves and place the other 2 egg yolk halves in the tuna mixture and stir with a rubber spatula until well blended. Spoon equal amounts of the tuna mixture in each of the egg halves.
4. Serve immediately, or cover with plastic wrap and refrigerate up to 24 hours.

Nutrition Info:

- Info90 cal., 4g fat (1g sag. fat), 105mg chol, 240mg sod., 3g carb (2g sugars, 0g fiber), 9g pro.

Tomato-jalapeno Granita

Servings:6
Cooking Time: 15 Minutes
Ingredients:

- 2 cups tomato juice
- 1/3 cup sugar
- 4 mint sprigs
- 1 jalapeno pepper, sliced
- 2 tablespoons lime juice
- Fresh mint leaves, optional

Directions:

1. In a small saucepan, bring the tomato juice, sugar, mint sprigs and jalapeno to a boil. Cook and stir until sugar is dissolved. Remove from the heat; cover and let stand 15 minutes.
2. Strain and discard solids. Stir in lime juice. Transfer to a 1-qt. dish; cool to room temperature. Freeze for 1 hour; stir with a fork.
3. Freeze 2-3 hours longer or until completely frozen, stirring every 30 minutes. Scrape granita with a fork just before serving; spoon into dessert dishes. If desired garnish with additional mint leaves.

Nutrition Info:

- Info59 cal., 0 fat (0 sat. fat), 0 chol., 205mg sod., 15g carb. (13g sugars, 0 fiber), 1g pro.

Mocha Pumpkin Seeds

Servings:3
Cooking Time: 25 Minutes
Ingredients:

- 6 tablespoons sugar
- 2 tablespoons baking cocoa
- 1 tablespoon instant coffee granules
- 1 large egg white
- 2 cups salted shelled pumpkin seeds (pepitas)

Directions:

1. Preheat oven to 325°. Place sugar, cocoa and coffee granules in a small food processor; cover and pulse until finely ground.
2. In a bowl, whisk egg white until frothy. Stir in pumpkin seeds. Sprinkle with sugar mixture; toss to coat evenly. Spread in a single layer in a parchment paper-lined 15x10x1-in. baking pan.
3. Bake 20-25 minutes or until dry and no longer sticky, stirring seeds every 10 minutes. Cool completely in pan. Store in an airtight container.

Nutrition Info:

- Info142 cal., 10g fat (2g sat. fat), 0 chol., 55mg sod., 10g carb. (7g sugars, 1g fiber), 6g pro.

Pickled Shrimp With Basil

Servings:20
Cooking Time: 15 Minutes
Ingredients:

- 1/2 cup red wine vinegar
- 1/2 cup olive oil
- 2 teaspoons seafood seasoning
- 2 teaspoons stone-ground mustard
- 1 garlic clove, minced
- 2 pounds peeled and deveined cooked shrimp (31-40 per pound)
- 1 medium lemon, thinly sliced
- 1 medium lime, thinly sliced
- 1/2 medium red onion, thinly sliced
- 1/4 cup thinly sliced fresh basil
- 2 tablespoons capers, drained
- 1/4 cup minced fresh basil
- 1/2 teaspoon kosher salt
- 1/4 teaspoon coarsely ground pepper

Directions:

1. In a large bowl, whisk the first five ingredients. Add shrimp, lemon, lime, onion, sliced basil and capers; toss gently to coat. Refrigerate, covered, up to 8 hours, stirring occasionally.
2. Just before serving, stir minced basil, salt and pepper into the shrimp mixture. Serve with a slotted spoon.

Nutrition Info:

- Info64 cal., 2g fat (0 sat. fat), 69mg chol., 111mg sod., 1g carb. (0 sugars, 0 fiber), 9g pro.

Mango Avocado Spring Rolls

Servings: 8
Cooking Time: 40 Minutes
Ingredients:

- 4 ounces reduced-fat cream cheese
- 2 tablespoons lime juice
- 1 teaspoon Sriracha Asian hot chili sauce or 1/2 teaspoon hot pepper sauce
- 1 medium sweet red pepper, finely chopped
- 2/3 cup cubed avocado
- 3 green onions, thinly sliced
- 1/3 cup chopped fresh cilantro
- 8 round rice paper wrappers (8 inches)
- 1 medium mango, peeled and thinly sliced
- 2 cups alfalfa sprouts

Directions:

1. Mix cream cheese, lime juice and chili sauce; gently stir in pepper, avocado, green onions and cilantro.
2. Fill a large shallow dish partway with water. Dip a rice paper wrapper into water just until pliable, about 45 seconds (do not soften completely); allow excess water to drip off.
3. Place wrapper on a flat surface. Place cream cheese mixture, mango and sprouts across bottom third of wrapper. Fold in both ends of wrapper; fold bottom side over filling, then roll up tightly. Place on a serving plate, seam side down. Repeat with remaining ingredients. Serve immediately.

Nutrition Info:

- Info117 cal., 5g fat (2g sat. fat), 10mg chol., 86mg sod., 16g carb. (6g sugars, 2g fiber), 3g pro.

Baby Carrots And Spicy Cream Dip

Servings: 4
Cooking Time: 5 Minutes
Ingredients:

- 1/3 cup fat-free sour cream
- 3 tablespoons reduced-fat tub-style cream cheese
- 3/4 teaspoon hot pepper sauce
- 1/8 teaspoon salt
- 48 baby carrots

Directions:

1. Stir the sour cream, cream cheese, pepper sauce, and salt together until well blended.
2. Let stand at least 10 minutes to develop flavors and mellow slightly. Serve with carrots.

Nutrition Info:

- Info90 cal., 2g fat (1g sag. fat), 10mg chol, 240mg sod., 16g carb (7g sugars, 3g fiber), 3g pro.

Asian Marinated Mushrooms

Servings: 4
Cooking Time: 8 Minutes
Ingredients:

- 8 ounces whole medium mushrooms, stemmed and wiped clean with damp paper towel
- 1/4 tablespoons lite soy sauce
- 2 tablespoons lime juice
- 1 teaspoon extra virgin olive oil

Directions:

1. Place the mushrooms, soy sauce, lime juice, and oil in a large plastic zippered bag. Seal the bag and shake to coat completely. Let stand 30 minutes. Meanwhile, preheat the broiler.
2. Place mushroom mixture (with marinade) in an 8-inch pie pan or baking pan and broil 4 inches away from heat source for 8 minutes or until the mushrooms begin to brown, stirring frequently.
3. Serve with wooden toothpicks and marinade. Top with 2 tablespoons chopped fresh parsley, if desired.

Nutrition Info:

- Info30 cal., 1g fat (0g sag. fat), 0mg chol, 240mg sod., 3g carb (1g sugars, 1g fiber), 2g pro.

Poultry Recipes

Turkey & Apricot Wraps

Servings:4
Cooking Time: 15 Minutes
Ingredients:
- 1/2 cup reduced-fat cream cheese
- 3 tablespoons apricot preserves
- 4 whole wheat tortillas (8 inches), room temperature
- 1/2 pound sliced reduced-sodium deli turkey
- 2 cups fresh baby spinach or arugula

Directions:
1. In a small bowl, mix cream cheese and preserves. Spread about 2 tablespoons over each tortilla to within 1/2 in. of edges. Layer with turkey and spinach. Roll up tightly. Serve immediately or wrap in plastic wrap and refrigerate until serving.

Nutrition Info:
- Info312 cal., 10g fat (4g sat. fat), 41mg chol., 655mg sod., 33g carb. (8g sugars, 2g fiber), 20g pro.

Weeknight Skillet Roast Chicken

Servings:4
Cooking Time:35 Minutes
Ingredients:
- 1 (4-pound) whole chicken, giblets discarded
- 1 tablespoon canola oil
- ½ teaspoon kosher salt
- ½ teaspoon pepper
- Lemon wedges

Directions:
1. Adjust oven rack to middle position, place 12-inch oven-safe skillet on rack, and heat oven to 450 degrees. Pat chicken dry with paper towels. Rub entire surface with oil and sprinkle with salt and pepper. Tie legs together with twine and tuck wing tips behind back.
2. Transfer chicken breast side up to hot skillet in oven. Roast chicken until breast registers 120 degrees and thighs register 135 degrees, 25 to 35 minutes. Turn oven off and leave chicken in oven until breast registers 160 degrees and thighs register 175 degrees, 25 to 35 minutes.
3. Transfer chicken to carving board and let rest for 20 minutes. Carve chicken, discard skin, and serve with lemon wedges.

Nutrition Info:
- Info240 cal., 6g fat (1g sag. fat), 160mg chol, 280mg sod., 0g carb (0g sugars, 0g fiber), 42g pro.

Chicken Strips Milano

Servings:6
Cooking Time: 20 Minutes
Ingredients:

- 12 ounces linguine
- 1 tablespoon minced garlic
- 4 1/2 teaspoons plus 2 tablespoons olive oil, divided
- 3/4 teaspoon dried parsley flakes
- 3/4 teaspoon pepper, divided

- 1/4 cup all-purpose flour
- 1 teaspoon dried basil
- 1/2 teaspoon salt
- 2 large eggs
- 1 1/2 pounds boneless skinless chicken breasts, cut into strips

Directions:

1. Cook the linguine according to package directions.
2. Meanwhile, in a large skillet, saute garlic in 4 1/2 teaspoons oil for 1 minute. Stir in parsley and 1/2 teaspoon pepper. Remove to a small bowl and set aside.
3. In a shallow bowl, combine the flour, basil, salt and remaining pepper. In another shallow bowl, whisk the eggs. Dredge chicken strips in flour mixture, then dip in eggs.
4. In the same skillet, cook and stir chicken in remaining oil over medium-high heat for 8-10 minutes or until no longer pink.
5. Drain linguine; place on a serving platter. Pour garlic mixture over linguine and toss to coat; top with chicken.

Nutrition Info:

- Info441 cal., 14g fat (3g sat. fat), 133mg chol., 278mg sod., 46g carb. (2g sugars, 2g fiber), 33g pro.

Chicken Piccata

Servings:4
Cooking Time:25 Minutes
Ingredients:

- ¼ cup plus 1 teaspoon all-purpose flour
- 8 (3-ounce) chicken cutlets, ¼ inch thick, trimmed of all visible fat
- ⅛ teaspoon salt
- ⅛ teaspoon pepper
- 2 tablespoons canola oil
- 2 tablespoons capers, rinsed
- 2 garlic cloves, minced
- 1 cup unsalted chicken broth
- ½ cup dry white wine
- 4 (2-inch) strips lemon zest plus 4 teaspoons juice
- 1 tablespoon unsalted butter, chilled

Directions:

1. Spread ¼ cup flour in shallow dish. Pat chicken cutlets dry with paper towels and sprinkle with salt and pepper. Working with 1 cutlet at a time, lightly dredge one side in flour, shaking off excess.
2. Heat 1 tablespoon oil in 12-inch skillet over medium heat until shimmering. Place 4 cutlets floured side down in skillet and cook until golden brown on first side, about 3 minutes. Flip cutlets and cook until no longer pink, about 1 minute. Transfer cutlets to large plate and tent with aluminum foil. Repeat with remaining 1 tablespoon oil and remaining 4 cutlets; transfer to plate and tent with foil.
3. Add capers and garlic to oil left in skillet and cook over medium heat until fragrant, about 30 seconds. Stir in remaining 1 teaspoon flour and cook for 1 minute. Slowly whisk in broth, wine, and lemon zest, scraping up any browned bits and smoothing out any lumps. Bring to simmer and cook sauce until thickened slightly and measures about ½ cup, 10 to 15 minutes.
4. Discard lemon zest. Nestle chicken into sauce along with any accumulated juices and cook until heated through, about 30 seconds. Transfer chicken to serving dish. Off heat, whisk lemon juice and butter into sauce until combined. Spoon sauce evenly over each cutlet before serving.

Nutrition Info:

- Info340 cal., 14g fat (3g sag. fat), 130mg chol, 280mg sod., 5g carb (1g sugars, 1g fiber), 40g pro.

Asian Lettuce Wraps

Servings:4
Cooking Time: 25 Minutes
Ingredients:

- 1 tablespoon canola oil
- 1 pound lean ground turkey
- 1 jalapeno pepper, seeded and minced
- 2 green onions, thinly sliced
- 2 garlic cloves, minced
- 2 tablespoons minced fresh basil
- 2 tablespoons lime juice
- 2 tablespoons reduced-sodium soy sauce
- 1 to 2 tablespoons chili garlic sauce
- 1 tablespoon sugar or sugar substitute blend equivalent to 1 tablespoon sugar
- 12 Bibb or Boston lettuce leaves
- 1 medium cucumber, julienned
- 1 medium carrot, julienned
- 2 cups bean sprouts

Directions:

1. In a skillet, heat oil over medium heat. Add turkey; cook 6-8 minutes or until no longer pink, breaking into crumbles. Add jalapeno, green onions and garlic; cook 2 minute longer. Stir in basil, lime juice, soy sauce, chili garlic sauce and sugar; heat through.
2. To serve, place turkey mixture in lettuce leaves; top with cucumber, carrot and bean sprouts. Fold lettuce over filling.

Nutrition Info:

- Info259 cal., 12g fat (3g sat. fat), 78mg chol., 503mg sod., 12g carb. (6g sugars, 3g fiber), 26g pro.

Italian Sausage & Provolone Skewers

Servings:8
Cooking Time: 30 Minutes
Ingredients:

- 1 large onion
- 1 large sweet red pepper
- 1 large green pepper
- 2 cups cherry tomatoes
- 1 tablespoon olive oil
- 1/2 teaspoon pepper
- 1/4 teaspoon salt
- 2 packages (12 ounces each) fully cooked Italian chicken sausage links, cut into 1 1/4-inch slices
- 16 cubes provolone cheese (3/4 inch each)

Directions:

1. Cut onion and peppers into 1-in. pieces; place in a large bowl. Add the tomatoes, oil, pepper and salt; toss to coat. On 16 metal or soaked wooden skewers, alternately thread sausage and vegetables.
2. Grill, covered, over medium heat 8-10 minutes or until sausage is heated through and vegetables are tender, turning occasionally. Remove kabobs from grill; thread one cheese cube onto each kabob.

Nutrition Info:

- Info220 cal., 13g fat (5g sat. fat), 75mg chol., 682mg sod., 7g carb. (3g sugars, 2g fiber), 20g pro.

Mediterranean Chicken Pasta

Servings:8
Cooking Time: 20 Minutes
Ingredients:

- 1 package (12 ounces) uncooked tricolor spiral pasta
- 2 tablespoons olive oil, divided
- 1 pound boneless skinless chicken breasts, cut into 1/2-inch pieces
- 1 large sweet red pepper, chopped
- 1 medium onion, chopped
- 3 garlic cloves, peeled and thinly sliced
- 1 cup white wine or reduced-sodium chicken broth
- 1/4 cup julienned soft sun-dried tomatoes (not packed in oil)
- 1 teaspoon dried basil
- 1 teaspoon Italian seasoning
- 1/2 teaspoon salt
- 1/4 teaspoon crushed red pepper flakes
- 1/4 teaspoon pepper
- 1 can (14 1/2 ounces) reduced-sodium chicken broth
- 1 can (14 ounces) water-packed quartered artichoke hearts, drained
- 1 package (6 ounces) fresh baby spinach
- 1 cup (4 ounces) crumbled feta cheese
- Thinly sliced fresh basil leaves and shaved Parmesan cheese, optional

Directions:

1. Cook pasta according to package directions. In a 6-qt. stockpot, heat 1 tablespoon oil over medium-high heat. Add chicken; cook and stir 4-6 minutes or until no longer pink. Remove from the pot.
2. In the same pot, heat remaining oil over medium heat. Add red pepper and onion; cook and stir for 4-5 minutes or until onion is tender. Add garlic; cook 1 minute longer. Add wine, sun-dried tomatoes and seasonings; bring to a boil. Reduce heat; simmer 5 minutes, stirring to loosen browned bits from the pot.
3. Add broth and artichoke hearts; return to a boil. Stir in spinach and chicken; cook just until spinach wilts.
4. Drain pasta; stir into the chicken mixture. Stir in feta cheese. If desired, top servings with the basil leaves and Parmesan cheese.

Nutrition Info:

- Info357 cal., 8g fat (2g sat. fat), 39mg chol., 609mg sod., 42g carb. (4g sugars, 4g fiber), 23g pro.

Wild Rice Salad

Servings:4
Cooking Time: 1 1/4 Hours
Ingredients:

- 3 cups water
- 1 cup uncooked wild rice
- 2 chicken bouillon cubes
- 4 1/2 teaspoons butter
- 1 cup cut fresh green beans
- 1 cup cubed cooked chicken breast
- 1 medium tomato, chopped
- 1 bunch green onions, sliced
- 1/4 cup rice vinegar
- 1 tablespoon sesame oil
- 1 garlic clove, minced
- 1/2 teaspoon dried tarragon
- 1/4 teaspoon pepper

Directions:

1. In a large saucepan, bring water, rice, bouillon and butter to a boil. Reduce heat; cover and simmer for 45-60 minutes or until rice is tender. Drain if necessary; transfer to a large bowl and cool completely.
2. Place the green beans in a steamer basket; place in a small saucepan over 1 in. of water. Bring to a boil; cover and steam for 8-10 minutes or until beans are crisp-tender.
3. Add chicken, tomato, onions and green beans to the rice; stir until blended. Combine the remaining ingredients; drizzle over mixture and toss to coat. Refrigerate until chilled.

Nutrition Info:

- Info330 cal., 10g fat (4g sat. fat), 39mg chol., 618mg sod., 43g carb. (3g sugars, 4g fiber), 18g pro.

Chicken Cucumber Boats

Servings:2
Cooking Time: 15 Minutes
Ingredients:

- 2 medium cucumbers
- 1/2 cup fat-free plain Greek yogurt
- 2 tablespoons mayonnaise
- 1/2 teaspoon garlic salt
- 3 teaspoons snipped fresh dill, divided
- 1 cup chopped cooked chicken breast
- 1 cup chopped seeded tomato (about 1 large), divided
- 1/2 cup fresh or frozen peas, thawed

Directions:

1. Cut each cucumber lengthwise in half; scoop out pulp, leaving a 1/4-in. shell. In a bowl, mix yogurt, mayonnaise, garlic salt and 1 teaspoon dill; gently stir in chicken, 3/4 cup tomato and peas.
2. Spoon into cucumber shells. Top with the remaining tomato and dill.

Nutrition Info:

- Info322 cal., 13g fat (2g sat. fat), 59mg chol.,398mg sod., 18g carb. (10g sugars, 6g fiber), 34g pro.

Italian Spaghetti With Chicken & Roasted Vegetables

Servings:6
Cooking Time: 25 Minutes
Ingredients:

- 3 plum tomatoes, seeded and chopped
- 2 medium zucchini, cubed
- 1 medium yellow summer squash, cubed
- 2 tablespoons olive oil, divided
- 2 teaspoons Italian seasoning, divided
- 8 ounces uncooked whole wheat spaghetti
- 1 pound boneless skinless chicken breasts, cubed
- 1/2 teaspoon garlic powder
- 1/2 cup reduced-sodium chicken broth
- 1/3 cup dry red wine or additional reduced-sodium chicken broth
- 4 cans (8 ounces each) no-salt-added tomato sauce
- 1 can (6 ounces) tomato paste
- 1/4 cup minced fresh basil
- 2 tablespoons minced fresh oregano
- 1/4 teaspoon salt
- 6 tablespoons shredded Parmesan cheese

Directions:

1. Preheat oven to 425°. In a large bowl, combine tomatoes, zucchini and squash. Add 1 tablespoon oil and 1 teaspoon Italian seasoning. Transfer to a 15x10x1-in. baking pan coated with cooking spray. Bake 15-20 minutes or until tender.
2. Meanwhile, cook the spaghetti according to package directions. Sprinkle chicken with garlic powder and remaining Italian seasoning. In a large nonstick skillet, heat remaining oil over medium heat. Add chicken; cook until no longer pink. Remove from skillet.
3. Add broth and wine to skillet, stirring to loosen browned bits from pan. Stir in the tomato sauce, tomato paste, basil, oregano and salt. Bring to a boil. Return chicken to skillet. Reduce heat; simmer, covered, 4-6 minutes or until sauce is slightly thickened.
4. Drain spaghetti. Add spaghetti and vegetables to the tomato mixture; heat through. Sprinkle with cheese.

Nutrition Info:

- Info379 cal., 9g fat (2g sat. fat), 45mg chol., 345mg sod., 49g carb. (14g sugars, 8g fiber), 26g pro.

Chicken Apple Sausage And Onion Smothered Grits

Servings: 4
Cooking Time:10 Minutes
Ingredients:
- 2/3 cup dry quick cooking grits
- 8 ounces sliced fresh mushrooms
- 3 (4 ounces each) links fully cooked chicken apple sausage, thinly sliced, such as Al Fresco
- 1 1/2 cups chopped onion

Directions:
1. Bring 2 2/3 cups water to a boil in a medium saucepan. Slowly stir in the grits, reduce heat to medium-low, cover, and cook 5–7 minutes or until thickened.
2. Meanwhile, heat a large skillet coated with cooking spray over medium-high heat. Add the mushrooms and cook 4 minutes or until beginning to lightly brown. Set aside on separate plate.
3. Coat skillet with cooking spray and cook sausage 3 minutes or until browned on edges, stirring occasionally. Set aside with mushrooms. To pan residue, add onions, coat with cooking spray, and cook 4 minutes or until richly browned. Add the sausage and mushrooms back to the skillet with any accumulated juices and 1/4 cup water. Cook 1 minute to heat through.
4. Sprinkle with 1/8 teaspoon salt and 1/8 teaspoon pepper. Spoon equal amounts of the grits in each of 4 shallow soup bowls, top with the sausage mixture.

Nutrition Info:
- Info270 cal., 7g fat (1g sag. fat), 60mg chol, 430mg sod., 31g carb (4g sugars, 3g fiber), 19g pro.

Roasted Chicken Thighs With Peppers & Potatoes

Servings:8
Cooking Time: 35 Minutes
Ingredients:
- 2 pounds red potatoes (about 6 medium)
- 2 large sweet red peppers
- 2 large green peppers
- 2 medium onions
- 2 tablespoons olive oil, divided
- 4 teaspoons minced fresh thyme or 1 1/2 teaspoons dried thyme, divided
- 3 teaspoons minced fresh rosemary or 1 teaspoon dried rosemary, crushed, divided
- 8 boneless skinless chicken thighs (about 2 pounds)
- 1/2 teaspoon salt
- 1/4 teaspoon pepper

Directions:
1. Preheat oven to 450°. Cut potatoes, peppers and onions into 1-in. pieces. Place the vegetables in a roasting pan. Drizzle with 1 tablespoon oil; sprinkle with 2 teaspoons each of thyme and rosemary; toss to coat. Place chicken over vegetables. Brush chicken with remaining oil; sprinkle with remaining thyme and rosemary. Sprinkle the vegetables and chicken thighs with salt and pepper.
2. Roast 35-40 minutes or until a thermometer inserted in chicken reads 170° and vegetables are tender.

Nutrition Info:
- Info308 cal., 12g fat (3g sat. fat), 76mg chol., 221mg sod., 25g carb. (5g sugars, 4g fiber), 24g pro.

Stovetop Tarragon Chicken

Servings:4
Cooking Time: 30 Minutes

Ingredients:

- 4 boneless skinless chicken breast halves (5 ounces each)
- 2 teaspoons paprika
- 1 tablespoon olive oil
- 1 package (10 ounces) julienned carrots
- 1/2 pound sliced fresh mushrooms
- 2 cans (10 3/4 ounces each) reduced-fat reduced-sodium condensed cream of chicken soup, undiluted
- 3 teaspoons dried tarragon
- 1 tablespoon lemon juice
- 3 small zucchini, thinly sliced

Directions:

1. Sprinkle chicken with paprika. In a Dutch oven, heat oil over medium heat. Cook chicken 2 minutes on each side or until lightly browned; remove from pan.
2. Add carrots and mushrooms to the same pan; cook, covered, 6-8 minutes or until carrots are crisp-tender, stirring occasionally. In a small bowl, mix soup, tarragon and lemon juice until blended; pour over vegetables. Return chicken to pan. Bring to a boil; reduce heat to low. Cook, covered, 8 minutes. Top with zucchini; cook, covered, 6-8 minutes longer or until a thermometer inserted in chicken reads 165° and vegetables are tender.

Nutrition Info:

- Info345 cal., 11g fat (3g sat. fat), 85mg chol., 649mg sod., 28g carb. (16g sugars, 5g fiber), 35g pro.

Apple-glazed Chicken Thighs

Servings:6
Cooking Time: 25 Minutes

Ingredients:

- 6 boneless skinless chicken thighs (1 1/2 pounds)
- 3/4 teaspoon seasoned salt
- 1/4 teaspoon pepper
- 1 tablespoon canola oil
- 1 cup unsweetened apple juice
- 1 teaspoon minced fresh thyme or 1/4 teaspoon dried thyme

Directions:

1. Sprinkle chicken with seasoned salt and pepper. In a large skillet, heat oil over medium-high heat. Brown chicken on both sides. Remove from pan.
2. Add juice and thyme to skillet. Bring to a boil, stirring to loosen browned bits from pan; cook until liquid is reduced by half. Return chicken to the pan; cook, covered, over medium heat 3-4 minutes longer or until a thermometer inserted in chicken reads 170°.

Nutrition Info:

- Info204 cal., 11g fat (2g sat. fat), 76mg chol., 255mg sod., 5g carb. (4g sugars, 0 fiber), 21g pro.

Fish & Seafood Recipes

Seared Scallops With Orange-lime Dressing

Servings:4

Cooking Time: 10 Minutes

Ingredients:

- 1½ pounds large sea scallops, tendons removed
- ⅛ teaspoon salt
- ⅛ teaspoon pepper
- 6 tablespoons extra-virgin olive oil
- 2 tablespoons orange juice
- 2 tablespoons lime juice
- 1 small shallot, minced
- 1 tablespoon minced fresh cilantro
- ⅛ teaspoon red pepper flakes

Directions:

1. Place scallops in rimmed baking sheet lined with clean kitchen towel. Place second clean kitchen towel on top of scallops and press gently on towel to blot liquid. Let scallops sit at room temperature, covered with towel, for 10 minutes. Sprinkle scallops with salt and pepper.

2. Whisk ¼ cup oil, orange juice, lime juice, shallot, cilantro, and pepper flakes together in bowl. Set aside for serving.

3. Heat 1 tablespoon oil in 12-inch nonstick skillet over medium-high heat until just smoking. Add half of scallops to skillet and cook, without moving them, until well browned on first side, about 1½ minutes. Flip scallops and continue to cook, without moving them, until well browned on second side, sides are firm, and centers are opaque, about 1½ minutes. Transfer scallops to serving platter and tent loosely with aluminum foil. Repeat with remaining 1 tablespoon oil and remaining scallops. Whisk dressing to recombine and serve with scallops.

Nutrition Info:

- Info310 cal., 22g fat (3g sag. fat), 40mg chol, 350mg sod., 7g carb (1g sugars, 0g fiber), 21g pro.

Tuna & White Bean Lettuce Wraps

Servings:4

Cooking Time: 20 Minutes

Ingredients:

- 1 can (12 ounces) light tuna in water, drained and flaked
- 1 can (15 ounces) cannellini beans, rinsed and drained
- 1/4 cup chopped red onion
- 2 tablespoons olive oil
- 1 tablespoon minced fresh parsley
- 1/8 teaspoon salt
- 1/8 teaspoon pepper
- 12 Bibb or Boston lettuce leaves (about 1 medium head)
- 1 medium ripe avocado, peeled and cubed

Directions:

1. In a small bowl, combine the first seven ingredients; toss lightly to combine. Serve tuna mixture in lettuce leaves; top with avocado.

Nutrition Info:

- Info279 cal., 13g fat (2g sat. fat), 31mg chol., 421mg sod., 19g carb. (1g sugars, 7g fiber), 22g pro.

Red Snapper With Fresh Tomato-basil Sauce

Servings: 4
Cooking Time:12–15 Minutes
Ingredients:

* 4 (4-ounce) snapper filets (or any mild, lean white fish filets), rinsed and patted dry
* 1/4 teaspoon salt (divided use)
* 1/8 teaspoon black pepper
* 1 pint grape tomatoes, quartered (2 cups total)
* 2 tablespoons chopped fresh basil
* 2 ounces crumbled, reduced-fat, sun-dried tomato and basil feta cheese

Directions:
1. Preheat the oven to 400°F.
2. Line a baking sheet with foil and coat with nonstick cooking spray. Arrange the filets on the foil about 2 inches apart. Sprinkle them evenly with 1/4 teaspoon salt and the pepper. Bake 12–15 minutes or until the filets are opaque in the center.
3. Combine the tomatoes, basil, and 1/4 teaspoon salt in a small saucepan. Cook over medium-high heat for 2 minutes or until the tomatoes are limp.
4. Place the filets on a serving platter, spoon the tomatoes evenly over the filets, and sprinkle each with feta.
Nutrition Info:

* Info160 cal., 4g fat (2g sag. fat), 50mg chol, 360mg sod., 5g carb (2g sugars, 2g fiber), 27g pro.

Cajun Baked Catfish

Servings:2
Cooking Time: 25 Minutes
Ingredients:

* 2 tablespoons yellow cornmeal
* 2 teaspoons Cajun or blackened seasoning
* 1/2 teaspoon dried thyme
* 1/2 teaspoon dried basil
* 1/4 teaspoon garlic powder
* 1/4 teaspoon lemon-pepper seasoning
* 2 catfish or tilapia fillets (6 ounces each)
* 1/4 teaspoon paprika

Directions:
1. Preheat oven to 400°. In a shallow bowl, mix the first six ingredients.
2. Dip the fillets in cornmeal mixture to evenly coat both sides. Place them on a baking sheet coated with cooking spray. Sprinkle with paprika.
3. Bake 20-25 minutes or until fish just begins to flake easily with a fork.
Nutrition Info:

* Info242 cal., 10g fat (2g sat. fat), 94mg chol., 748mg sod., 8g carb. (0 sugars, 1g fiber), 27g pro.

Nut-crusted Cod Fillets

Servings:4
Cooking Time:50 Minutes
Ingredients:

- ½ cup shelled unsalted pistachios
- 2 tablespoons canola oil
- 1 large shallot, minced
- Salt and pepper
- 1 garlic clove, minced
- 1 teaspoon minced fresh thyme or ¼ teaspoon dried
- ½ cup 100 percent whole-wheat panko bread crumbs
- 2 tablespoons minced fresh parsley
- 1 tablespoon plain low-fat yogurt
- 1 large egg yolk
- ½ teaspoon grated lemon zest, plus lemon wedges for serving
- 4 (6-ounce) skinless cod fillets, 1 to 1½ inches thick

Directions:

1. Adjust oven rack to middle position and heat oven to 300 degrees. Set wire rack in rimmed baking sheet and spray lightly with canola oil spray. Process pistachios in food processor until finely chopped, 20 to 30 seconds. Heat oil in 12-inch nonstick skillet over medium heat until shimmering. Add shallot and ⅛ teaspoon salt and cook until softened, about 3 minutes. Stir in garlic and thyme and cook until fragrant, about 30 seconds. Reduce heat to medium-low and add pistachios, panko, and ¼ teaspoon pepper. Cook, stirring frequently, until well browned and crisp, about 8 minutes. Transfer nut mixture to shallow dish and let cool for 10 minutes. Stir in parsley.
2. Whisk yogurt, egg yolk, and lemon zest together in bowl. Pat cod dry with paper towels and sprinkle with ¼ teaspoon salt and ⅛ teaspoon pepper. Brush tops of fillets evenly with yogurt mixture. Working with 1 fillet at a time, dredge brushed side in nut mixture, pressing gently to adhere.
3. Transfer cod, crumb side up, to prepared rack and bake until cod flakes apart when gently prodded with paring knife and registers 140 degrees, 20 to 25 minutes, rotating sheet halfway through baking. Carefully transfer fish to individual serving plates and serve with lemon wedges.

Nutrition Info:

- Info290 cal., 13g fat (1g sag. fat), 120mg chol, 320mg sod., 8g carb (2g sugars, 2g fiber), 34g pro.

Garlic Tilapia With Spicy Kale

Servings:4
Cooking Time: 30 Minutes
Ingredients:

- 3 tablespoons olive oil, divided
- 2 garlic cloves, minced
- 1 teaspoon fennel seed
- 1/2 teaspoon crushed red pepper flakes
- 1 bunch kale, trimmed and coarsely chopped (about 16 cups)
- 2/3 cup water
- 4 tilapia fillets (6 ounces each)
- 3/4 teaspoon pepper, divided
- 1/2 teaspoon garlic salt
- 1 can (15 ounces) cannellini beans, rinsed and drained
- 1/2 teaspoon salt

Directions:

1. In 6-qt. stockpot, heat 1 tablespoon oil over medium heat. Add garlic, fennel and pepper flakes; cook and stir for 1 minute. Add kale and water; bring to a boil. Reduce heat; simmer, covered, 10-12 minutes or until the kale is tender.
2. Meanwhile, sprinkle tilapia with 1/2 teaspoon pepper and garlic salt. In large skillet, heat remaining oil over medium heat. Add tilapia; cook 3-4 minutes per side or until fish flakes easily with fork.
3. Add beans, salt and the remaining pepper to kale; heat through, stirring occasionally. Serve with tilapia.

Nutrition Info:

- Info359 cal., 13g fat (2g sat. fat), 83mg chol., 645mg sod., 24g carb. (0 sugars, 6g fiber), 39g pro.

Grilled Swordfish With Eggplant, Tomato, And Chickpea Salad

Servings:4

Cooking Time:30minutes

Ingredients:

- 1 cup fresh cilantro leaves
- ½ red onion, chopped coarse
- 5 tablespoons extra-virgin olive oil
- 3 tablespoons lemon juice
- 4 garlic cloves, chopped
- 1 teaspoon ground cumin
- 1 teaspoon paprika
- ¼ teaspoon cayenne pepper
- ⅛ teaspoon ground cinnamon
- Salt and pepper
- 4 (6-ounce) skin-on swordfish steaks, 1 to 1½ inches thick
- 1 large eggplant, sliced into ½-inch-thick rounds
- 6 ounces cherry tomatoes, halved
- 1 (15-ounce) can no-salt added chickpeas, rinsed

Directions:

1. Process cilantro, onion, 3 tablespoons oil, lemon juice, garlic, cumin, paprika, cayenne, cinnamon, and ¼ teaspoon salt in food processor until smooth, about 2 minutes, scraping down sides of bowl as needed. Measure out and reserve ½ cup cilantro mixture. Transfer remaining cilantro mixture to large bowl and set aside.

2. Brush swordfish with reserved ½ cup cilantro mixture. Brush eggplant with remaining 2 tablespoons oil and sprinkle with ⅛ teaspoon salt and ⅛ teaspoon pepper.

3. FOR A CHARCOAL GRILL Open bottom vent completely. Light large chimney starter filled with charcoal briquettes (6 quarts). When top coals are partially covered with ash, pour two-thirds evenly over half of grill, then pour remaining coals over other half of grill. Set cooking grate in place, cover, and open lid vent completely. Heat grill until hot, about 5 minutes.

4. FOR A GAS GRILL Turn all burners to high, cover, and heat grill until hot, about 15 minutes. Leave primary burner on high and turn other burner(s) to medium-high.

5. Clean cooking grate, then repeatedly brush grate with well-oiled paper towels until black and glossy, 5 to 10 times. Place swordfish and eggplant on hotter part of grill. Cook swordfish, uncovered, until streaked with dark grill marks, 6 to 9 minutes, gently flipping steaks using 2 spatulas halfway through cooking. Cook eggplant, flipping as needed, until softened and lightly charred, about 8 minutes; transfer to bowl and cover with aluminum foil.

6. Gently move swordfish to cooler part of grill and continue to cook, uncovered, until swordfish flakes apart when gently prodded with paring knife and registers 140 degrees, 1 to 3 minutes per side; transfer to serving platter and tent loosely with foil.

7. Coarsely chop eggplant and add to bowl with cilantro mixture along with tomatoes and chickpeas. Gently toss to combine and season with pepper to taste. Serve.

Nutrition Info:

- Info530 cal., 30g fat (5g sag. fat), 110mg chol, 380mg sod., 25g carb (7g sugars, 8g fiber), 40g pro.

Cheesy Shrimp And Grits

Servings:4
Cooking Time:30 Minutes
Ingredients:

- 1 tablespoon extra-virgin olive oil
- 3 scallions, white parts sliced thin, green parts sliced thin on bias
- 2 garlic cloves, minced
- 1 teaspoon minced canned chipotle chile in adobo sauce
- 4 cups water
- ½ cup 1 percent low-fat milk
- Salt and pepper
- 1 cup old-fashioned grits
- 2 ounces sharp cheddar cheese, shredded (½ cup)
- 1½ pounds extra-large shrimp (21 to 25 per pound), peeled and deveined
- Lemon wedges

Directions:

1. Adjust oven rack to middle position and heat oven to 450 degrees. Heat oil in medium saucepan over medium heat until shimmering. Add scallion whites and cook until softened, about 2 minutes. Stir in garlic and chipotle and cook until fragrant, about 30 seconds. Stir in water, milk, and pinch salt and bring to boil. Slowly whisk in grits. Reduce heat to low and cook, stirring often, until grits are thick and creamy, about 15 minutes.

2. Off heat, stir in cheese, ⅛ teaspoon salt, and ⅛ teaspoon pepper, then transfer to 13 by 9-inch baking dish. Nestle shrimp into grits, leaving tails exposed. Bake until shrimp are cooked through, about 15 minutes. Let cool slightly, then sprinkle with scallion greens. Serve with lemon wedges.

Nutrition Info:

- Info330 cal., 10g fat (4g sag. fat), 175mg chol, 380mg sod., 32g carb (2g sugars, 3g fiber), 25g pro.

Halibut En Cocotte With Cherry Tomatoes

Servings:8
Cooking Time:40 Minutes
Ingredients:

- 2 tablespoons extra-virgin olive oil
- 2 garlic cloves, sliced thin
- ⅛ teaspoon red pepper flakes
- 12 ounces cherry tomatoes, quartered
- 1 tablespoon capers, rinsed
- 1 teaspoon minced fresh thyme or ¼ teaspoon dried
- 2 (1½-pound) skin-on full halibut steaks, 1 to 1½ inches thick and 10 to 12 inches long, trimmed of cartilage at both ends
- Salt and pepper

Directions:

1. Adjust oven rack to lowest position and heat oven to 250 degrees. Cook 1 tablespoon oil, garlic, and pepper flakes in Dutch oven over medium-low heat until garlic is light golden, 2 to 4 minutes. Off heat, stir in tomatoes, capers, and thyme.

2. Pat halibut steaks dry with paper towels and sprinkle with ⅛ teaspoon salt and ⅛ teaspoon pepper. Lay halibut on top of tomatoes in pot. Place large sheet of aluminum foil over pot and press to seal, then cover with lid. Transfer pot to oven and cook until halibut flakes apart when gently prodded with paring knife and registers 140 degrees, 35 to 40 minutes.

3. Gently transfer halibut to serving platter and tent loosely with foil. Simmer tomato mixture over medium-high heat until thickened slightly, about 2 minutes. Off heat, stir in remaining 1 tablespoon oil and season with pepper to taste. Spoon sauce evenly over halibut and serve.

Nutrition Info:

- Info170 cal., 5g fat (1g sag. fat), 70mg chol, 160mg sod., 2g carb (1g sugars, 1g fiber), 27g pro.

Lime-cilantro Tilapia

Servings:4
Cooking Time: 25 Minutes
Ingredients:
- 1/3 cup all-purpose flour
- 3/4 teaspoon salt
- 1/2 teaspoon pepper
- 1/2 teaspoon ground cumin, divided
- 4 tilapia fillets (6 ounces each)
- 1 tablespoon olive oil
- 1/2 cup reduced-sodium chicken broth
- 2 tablespoons minced fresh cilantro
- 1 teaspoon grated lime peel
- 2 tablespoons lime juice

Directions:
1. In a shallow bowl, mix flour, salt, pepper and 1/4 teaspoon cumin. Dip fillets in flour mixture to coat both sides; shake off excess.
2. In a large nonstick skillet, heat oil over medium heat. Add fillets; cook, uncovered, 3-4 minutes on each side or until the fish flakes easily with a fork. Remove and keep warm.
3. To the same pan, add broth, cilantro, lime peel, lime juice and the remaining cumin; bring to a boil. Reduce the heat; simmer, uncovered, 2-3 minutes or until slightly thickened. Serve with tilapia.

Nutrition Info:
- Info198 cal., 5g fat (1g sat. fat), 83mg chol., 398 mg sod., 6g carb. (1g sugars, 0 fiber), 33g pro.

Tartar Sauce

Servings:1
Cooking Time:30 Minutes
Ingredients:
- This briny sauce is the classic accompaniment for fish.
- ¼ cup mayonnaise
- 2 tablespoons low-fat sour cream
- 2 tablespoons finely chopped red onion
- 3 cornichons, minced, plus 2 teaspoons cornichon pickling juice
- 1 tablespoon capers, rinsed and minced
- Water
- Pepper

Directions:
1. Combine mayonnaise, sour cream, onion, cornichons and juice, and capers in bowl. Add water as needed to thin sauce consistency and season with pepper to taste. Cover and refrigerate for 30 minutes before serving. (Sauce can be refrigerated for up to 24 hours.)

Nutrition Info:
- Info100 cal., 11g fat (2g sag. fat), 5mg chol, 200mg sod., 2g carb (2g sugars, 0g fiber), 1g pro.

Creamy Chipotle Chile Sauce

Servings:1
Cooking Time:1week
Ingredients:

- You can vary the spiciness of this sauce by adjusting the amount of chipotle.
- ¼ cup mayonnaise
- 2 tablespoons low-fat sour cream
- 1 tablespoon lime juice
- 2 teaspoons minced fresh cilantro
- 1 garlic clove, minced
- ½ teaspoon minced canned chipotle chile in adobo sauce
- Water
- Pepper

Directions:
1. Combine mayonnaise, sour cream, lime juice, cilantro, garlic, and chipotle in bowl. Add water as needed to thin sauce consistency and season with pepper to taste. Cover and refrigerate for 30 minutes before serving. (Sauce can be refrigerated for up to 24 hours.)

Nutrition Info:
- Info100 cal., 11g fat (2g sag. fat), 5mg chol, 95mg sod., 1g carb (1g sugars, 0g fiber), 1g pro.

No-fry Fish Fry

Servings: 4
Cooking Time:6 Minutes
Ingredients:

- 2 tablespoons yellow cornmeal
- 2 teaspoons Cajun seasoning
- 4 (4-ounce) tilapia filets (or any mild, lean white fish filets), rinsed and patted dry
- 1/8 teaspoon salt
- Lemon wedges (optional)

Directions:
1. Preheat the broiler.
2. Coat a broiler rack and pan with nonstick cooking spray and set aside.
3. Mix the cornmeal and Cajun seasoning thoroughly in a shallow pan, such as a pie plate. Coat each filet with nonstick cooking spray and coat evenly with the cornmeal mixture.
4. Place the filets on the rack and broil 6 inches away from the heat source for 3 minutes on each side.
5. Place the filets on a serving platter, sprinkle each evenly with salt, and serve with lemon wedges, if desired.

Nutrition Info:
- Info130 cal., 2g fat (0g sag. fat), 50mg chol, 250mg sod., 4g carb (0g sugars, 0g fiber), 23g pro.

Oven-roasted Salmon

Servings:4
Cooking Time:10 Minutes
Ingredients:

- 1 (1½-pound) skin-on salmon fillet, 1 inch thick
- 1 teaspoon extra-virgin olive oil
- ¼ teaspoon salt
- ⅛ teaspoon pepper

Directions:
1. Adjust oven rack to lowest position, place aluminum foil–lined rimmed baking sheet on rack, and heat oven to 500 degrees. Cut salmon crosswise into 4 fillets, then make 4 or 5 shallow slashes about an inch apart along skin side of each piece, being careful not to cut into flesh. Pat fillets dry with paper towels, rub with oil, and sprinkle with salt and pepper.
2. Once oven reaches 500 degrees, reduce oven temperature to 275 degrees. Remove sheet from oven and carefully place salmon, skin-side down, on hot sheet. Roast until centers are still translucent when checked with tip of paring knife and register 125 degrees (for medium-rare), 4 to 6 minutes.
3. Slide spatula along underside of fillets and transfer to individual serving plates or serving platter, leaving skin behind; discard skin. Serve.

Nutrition Info:
- Info360 cal., 24g fat (5g sag. fat), 95mg chol, 250mg sod., 0g carb (0g sugars, 0g fiber), 35g pro.

Vegetarian Recipes

Cheese Manicotti

Servings:7
Cooking Time: 1 Hour
Ingredients:

- 1 carton (15 ounces) reduced-fat ricotta cheese
- 1/2 cup shredded part-skim mozzarella cheese
- 1 small onion, finely chopped
- 1 large egg, lightly beaten
- 2 tablespoons minced fresh parsley
- 1/2 teaspoon pepper
- 1/4 teaspoon salt
- 1 cup grated Parmesan cheese, divided
- 4 cups marinara sauce
- 1/2 cup water
- 1 package (8 ounces) manicotti shells

Directions:

1. Preheat oven to 350°. In a small bowl, mix the first seven ingredients; stir in 1/2 cup Parmesan cheese. In another bowl, mix marinara sauce and water; spread 3/4 cup sauce onto bottom of a 13x9-in. baking dish coated with cooking spray. Fill uncooked manicotti shells with ricotta mixture; arrange over sauce. Top with remaining sauce.
2. Bake, covered, 50 minutes or until pasta is tender. Sprinkle with remaining Parmesan cheese. Bake, uncovered, 10-15 minutes longer or until the cheese is melted.

Nutrition Info:

- Info340 cal., 8g fat (5g sat. fat), 60mg chol., 615mg sod., 46g carb. (16g sugars, 4g fiber), 19g pro.

Hurried Hummus Wraps

Servings: 4
Cooking Time: 5 Minutes
Ingredients:

- 4 whole-wheat flour tortillas
- 1/2 cup prepared hummus
- 6 cups packed mixed greens or spring greens
- 2 ounces crumbled reduced-fat feta or reduced-fat bleu cheese

Directions:

1. Warm tortillas according to package directions.
2. Top each with 2 tablespoons hummus, 1 1/2 cups lettuce, and 2 tablespoons cheese, roll tightly and cut in half.

Nutrition Info:

- Info210 cal., 14g fat (2g sag. fat), 5mg chol, 420mg sod., 28g carb (1g sugars, 4g fiber), 8g pro.

Thai-style Red Curry With Cauliflower

Servings:4
Cooking Time:10 Minutes
Ingredients:

- 1 (13.5-ounce) can light coconut milk
- 1 tablespoon fish sauce
- 1 teaspoon grated lime zest plus 1 tablespoon juice
- 2 teaspoons Thai red curry paste
- ⅛ teaspoon red pepper flakes
- 2 tablespoons plus 1 teaspoon canola oil
- 2 garlic cloves, minced
- 1 teaspoon grated fresh ginger
- 1 large head cauliflower (3 pounds), cored and cut into ¾-inch florets
- ¼ cup fresh basil leaves, torn into rough ½-inch pieces

Directions:

1. Whisk coconut milk, fish sauce, lime zest and juice, curry paste, and pepper flakes together in bowl. In separate bowl, combine 1 teaspoon oil, garlic, and ginger.
2. Heat remaining 2 tablespoons oil in 12-inch nonstick skillet over high heat until shimmering. Add cauliflower and ¼ cup water, cover, and cook until cauliflower is just tender and translucent, about 5 minutes. Uncover and continue to cook, stirring occasionally, until liquid is evaporated and cauliflower is tender and well browned, 8 to 10 minutes.
3. Push cauliflower to sides of skillet. Add garlic mixture and cook, mashing mixture into skillet, until fragrant, about 30 seconds. Stir garlic mixture into cauliflower and reduce heat to medium-high. Whisk coconut milk mixture to recombine, add to skillet, and simmer until slightly thickened, about 4 minutes. Off heat, stir in basil. Serve.

Nutrition Info:

- Info200 cal., 13g fat (4g sag. fat), 0mg chol, 380mg sod., 20g carb (7g sugars, 7g fiber), 7g pro.

Garden Harvest Spaghetti Squash

Servings:4
Cooking Time: 35 Minutes
Ingredients:

- 1 medium spaghetti squash (about 4 pounds)
- 1 medium sweet red pepper, chopped
- 1 medium red onion, chopped
- 1 small zucchini, chopped
- 1 cup chopped fresh mushrooms
- 1/2 cup chopped leek (white portion only)
- 1/2 cup shredded carrots
- 1 tablespoon olive oil
- 1 garlic clove, minced
- 1 can (14 1/2 ounces) stewed tomatoes
- 1/2 cup tomato paste
- 1/4 cup V8 juice
- 1 teaspoon pepper
- 1/2 teaspoon salt
- 2 cups fresh baby spinach
- 1 tablespoon minced fresh basil
- 2 teaspoons minced fresh oregano
- 2 teaspoons minced fresh thyme
- 1 teaspoon minced fresh rosemary
- 1/4 cup grated Parmesan and Romano cheese blend

Directions:

1. Cut the squash in half lengthwise; discard seeds. Place squash cut side down in a 15x10x1-in. baking pan; add 1/2 in. of hot water. Bake, uncovered, at 375° for 30-40 minutes. Drain water from the pan; turn squash cut side up. Bake 5 minutes longer or until the squash is tender.
2. Meanwhile, in a Dutch oven, saute the red pepper, onion, zucchini, mushrooms, leek and carrots in oil until tender. Add garlic; cook for 1 minute longer. Add the stewed tomatoes, tomato paste, V8 juice, pepper and salt; bring to a boil. Reduce heat; cover and simmer for 15 minutes. Stir in spinach and herbs; heat through.
3. When squash is cool enough to handle, use a fork to separate strands. Serve with sauce; sprinkle with cheese.

Nutrition Info:

- Info270 cal., 8g fat (2g sat. fat), 8mg chol., 751mg sod., 47g carb. (13g sugars, 10g fiber), 10g pro.

Stir-fried Tofu With Shiitakes And Green Beans

Servings:4
Cooking Time:15 Minutes

Ingredients:

- SAUCE
- ¾ cup low-sodium vegetable broth
- 3 tablespoons low-sodium soy sauce
- 2 tablespoons rice vinegar
- 2 teaspoons cornstarch
- 1 tablespoon toasted sesame oil
- ⅛ teaspoon red pepper flakes
- STIR-FRY
- 14 ounces extra-firm tofu, cut into ¾-inch pieces
- 3 tablespoons cornstarch
- 3 tablespoons canola oil
- 2 scallions, white and green parts separated and sliced thin on bias
- 3 garlic cloves, minced
- 1 tablespoon grated fresh ginger
- 12 ounces green beans, trimmed and cut on bias into 1-inch lengths
- 12 ounces shiitake mushrooms, stemmed and quartered
- 1 tablespoon toasted sesame seeds (optional)

Directions:

1. FOR THE SAUCE Whisk all ingredients together in bowl.
2. FOR THE STIR-FRY Spread tofu on paper towel–lined baking sheet and let drain for 20 minutes. Gently pat dry with paper towels. Toss drained tofu with cornstarch in bowl.
3. Combine 1 teaspoon oil, scallion whites, garlic, and ginger in bowl. Heat 2 tablespoons oil in 12-inch nonstick skillet over high heat until shimmering. Add tofu and cook, turning as needed, until crisp and well browned on all sides, 12 to 15 minutes; transfer to paper towel–lined plate.
4. Add remaining 2 teaspoons oil to now-empty skillet and heat over medium-high heat until shimmering. Add green beans and mushrooms, cover, and cook until mushrooms release their liquid and green beans are bright green and beginning to soften, 4 to 5 minutes. Uncover and continue to cook until vegetables are spotty brown, about 3 minutes.
5. Push vegetables to sides of skillet. Add garlic mixture to center and cook, mashing mixture into skillet, until fragrant, about 30 seconds. Stir garlic mixture into vegetables, then stir in tofu. Whisk sauce to recombine, then add to skillet and cook, stirring constantly, until sauce is thickened, about 30 seconds. Transfer to serving platter and sprinkle with scallion greens and sesame seeds, if using. Serve.

Nutrition Info:

- Info310 cal., 21g fat (2g sag. fat), 0mg chol, 470mg sod., 19g carb (5g sugars, 4g fiber), 14g pro.

Cheesy Tortilla Rounds

Servings: 4
Cooking Time:14 Minutes

Ingredients:

- 4 (6-inch) soft corn tortillas
- 1 cup fat-free refried beans
- 1/2 cup shredded, reduced-fat mozzarella cheese
- 1 poblano chili pepper, seeded and thinly sliced, or 2 jalapeño chili peppers, seeded and thinly sliced

Directions:

1. Preheat the broiler.
2. Place a large nonstick skillet over medium-high heat until hot. Coat the skillet with nonstick cooking spray. Place two tortillas in the skillet and cook 1 minute or until they begin to lightly brown on the bottom. Turn them and cook 1 minute, then place on a baking sheet. Repeat with the other two tortillas.
3. Return the skillet to medium-high heat, coat with nonstick cooking spray, and add the peppers. Coat the peppers with nonstick cooking spray and cook 6 minutes or until they are tender and brown, stirring frequently. Remove them from the heat.
4. Spread equal amounts of beans evenly on each tortilla. Broil 4 inches away from the heat source for 1 minute. Sprinkle the cheese and pepper slices evenly over each tortilla and broil another 2 minutes or until the cheese has melted. Serve with lime wedges, if desired.

Nutrition Info:

- Info150 cal., 3g fat (1g sag. fat), 10mg chol, 370mg sod., 23g carb (2g sugars, 5g fiber), 9g pro.

Broccoli And Toasted Nut Pilaf

Servings: 5
Cooking Time:28 Minutes
Ingredients:

- 2/3 cup pecan pieces
- 1 (6-ounce) package long grain and wild rice with seasonings
- 2 cups frozen broccoli florets, thawed
- 2 cups frozen corn kernels, thawed
- 1/2 cup water
- 1/8 teaspoon salt
- 1/8 teaspoon black pepper

Directions:

1. Place a medium saucepan over medium heat until hot. Add the nuts and cook 2–3 minutes or until they begin to lightly brown and smell fragrant, stirring frequently. Place them on a plate and set aside.
2. Add the amount of water called for on the rice package to the saucepan. Bring to a boil, then add the rice and seasonings. Return to a boil, reduce the heat, cover tightly, and cook 20 minutes. Add the broccoli, corn, and water to the rice and stir. Cover and cook another 5 minutes or until the broccoli is just tender.
3. Remove the rice from the heat and add the pecans, salt, and pepper. Let stand 2–3 minutes if any liquid remains in the pot.

Nutrition Info:

- Info280 cal., 12g fat (1g sag. fat), 0mg chol, 450mg sod., 39g carb (4g sugars, 4g fiber), 7g pro.

Tasty Lentil Tacos

Servings:6
Cooking Time: 40 Minutes
Ingredients:

- 1 teaspoon canola oil
- 1 medium onion, finely chopped
- 1 garlic clove, minced
- 1 cup dried lentils, rinsed
- 1 tablespoon chili powder
- 2 teaspoons ground cumin
- 1 teaspoon dried oregano
- 2 1/2 cups vegetable or reduced-sodium chicken broth
- 1 cup salsa
- 12 taco shells
- 1 1/2 cups shredded lettuce
- 1 cup chopped fresh tomatoes
- 1 1/2 cups shredded reduced-fat cheddar cheese
- 6 tablespoons fat-free sour cream

Directions:

1. In a large nonstick skillet, heat oil over medium heat; saute onion and garlic until tender. Add the lentils and seasonings; cook and stir 1 minute. Stir in broth; bring to a boil. Reduce heat; simmer, covered, until lentils are tender, 25-30 minutes.
2. Cook, uncovered, until mixture is thickened, for 6-8 minutes, stirring occasionally. Mash lentils slightly; stir in salsa and heat through. Serve in taco shells. Top with remaining ingredients.

Nutrition Info:

- Info365 cal., 12g fat (5g sat. fat), 21mg chol., 777mg sod., 44g carb. (5g sugars, 6g fiber), 19g pro.

Country Vegetable And Thyme Quiche

Servings: 4
Cooking Time:35 Minutes
Ingredients:

- 1 pound frozen corn and vegetable blend (or your favorite vegetable blend), thawed
- 1/2 teaspoon dried thyme
- 1/4 teaspoon salt
- 1/4 teaspoon black pepper
- 1 1/2 cups egg substitute
- 1/2 cup shredded, reduced-fat, sharp cheddar cheese

Directions:

1. Preheat the oven to 350°F.
2. Coat a 9-inch deep-dish pie pan with nonstick cooking spray. Place the vegetables in the pan and sprinkle them evenly with thyme, salt, and pepper. Pour egg substitute over the vegetables and bake 35 minutes or until just set.
3. Remove the quiche from the oven, sprinkle evenly with the cheese, and let stand 10 minutes to melt the cheese and let the quiche set.

Nutrition Info:

- Info150 cal., 2g fat (1g sag. fat), 5mg chol, 430mg sod., 16g carb (4g sugars, 5g fiber), 16g pro.

Zucchini On Bleu Cheese Pasta

Servings: 4
Cooking Time:15 Minutes
Ingredients:

- 6 ounces uncooked whole-grain rotini pasta
- 2 medium zucchini squash
- 4 whole green onions, ends trimmed
- 2 ounces reduced-fat bleu cheese, crumbled
- 3/8 teaspoon salt, divided use
- 1/8 teaspoon pepper

Directions:

1. Cook pasta according to package directions. Drain and reserve 1/4 cup pasta water.
2. Meanwhile, heat a grill pan or skillet over medium-high heat. Cut zucchini in quarters lengthwise. Then cut each quarter in half crosswise (creating 8 pieces total). Coat the zucchini and green onions with cooking spray.
3. Cook zucchini 5 minutes, turning occasionally. Add the green onions and cook another 5 minutes or until zucchini is just tender, turning occasionally.
4. Toss pasta with the bleu cheese, reserved 1/4 cup pasta water, 1/4 teaspoon salt, and 1/8 teaspoon pepper. Top with the zucchini and onions. Top with 1/8 teaspoon salt.

Nutrition Info:

- Info210 cal., 3g fat (1g sag. fat), 10mg chol, 420mg sod., 38g carb (3g sugars, 2g fiber), 12g pro.

Stacked Vegetables & Ravioli

Servings:6
Cooking Time: 30 Minutes
Ingredients:

- 2 yellow summer squash
- 2 medium zucchini
- 1 package (9 ounces) refrigerated cheese ravioli
- 1 cup ricotta cheese
- 1 large egg
- 1/2 teaspoon garlic salt
- 1 jar (24 ounces) marinara or spaghetti sauce
- 10 fresh basil leaves, divided
- 3/4 cup shredded Parmesan cheese

Directions:

1. Preheat oven to 350°. Using a vegetable peeler, cut the squash and zucchini into very thin lengthwise strips. In a Dutch oven, cook ravioli according to package directions, adding vegetable strips during last 3 minutes of cooking.
2. Meanwhile, in a small bowl, combine the ricotta cheese, egg and garlic salt; set aside. Drain ravioli and vegetables.
3. Spread 1/2 cup marinara sauce into a greased 11x7-in. baking dish. Layer with half of the ravioli and vegetables, half of ricotta mixture, seven basil leaves and 1 cup marinara sauce. Layer with the remaining ravioli, vegetables and marinara sauce. Dollop the remaining ricotta mixture over top; sprinkle with Parmesan cheese.
4. Cover and bake 25 minutes. Uncover and bake 5-10 minutes longer or until cheese is melted. Let stand 10 minutes before cutting. Thinly slice remaining basil; sprinkle over top.

Nutrition Info:

- Info323 cal., 11g fat (6g sat. fat), 76mg chol., 779mg sod., 39g carb. (15g sugars, 4g fiber), 19g pro.

Summer Squash "spaghetti" With Roasted Cherry Tomato Sauce

Servings:4
Cooking Time:30 Minutes
Ingredients:

- 6 ounces (¾ cup) whole-milk ricotta cheese
- 6 tablespoons chopped fresh basil
- Salt and pepper
- 3 pounds yellow summer squash, trimmed
- 2 pounds cherry tomatoes, halved
- 1 shallot, sliced thin
- 3 tablespoons extra-virgin olive oil
- 5 garlic cloves, minced
- 1 tablespoon minced fresh oregano or 1 teaspoon dried
- 1 tablespoon no-salt-added tomato paste
- ¼ teaspoon red pepper flakes

Directions:

1. Adjust oven racks to upper-middle and lower-middle positions and heat oven to 375 degrees. Line rimmed baking sheet with aluminum foil. Combine ricotta, 2 tablespoons basil, ⅛ teaspoon salt, and ¼ teaspoon pepper in bowl; set aside for serving. Using spiralizer, cut squash into ⅛-inch-thick noodles, then cut noodles into 12-inch lengths.
2. Toss tomatoes, shallot, 2 tablespoons oil, garlic, oregano, tomato paste, pepper flakes, ⅛ teaspoon salt, and ¼ teaspoon pepper together in bowl. Spread tomato mixture in lined baking sheet and roast, without stirring, on lower rack until tomatoes are softened and skins begin to shrivel, about 30 minutes.
3. Meanwhile, toss squash with ⅛ teaspoon salt and remaining 1 tablespoon oil on second rimmed baking sheet and roast on upper rack until tender, 20 to 25 minutes. Transfer squash to colander and shake to remove any excess liquid; transfer to large serving bowl. (If tomatoes are not finished cooking, cover bowl with aluminum foil to keep warm.)
4. Add roasted tomato mixture and any accumulated juices to bowl with squash and gently toss to combine. Season with ⅛ teaspoon salt and pepper to taste. Dollop individual portions with 3 tablespoons ricotta mixture and sprinkle with remaining ¼ cup basil before serving.

Nutrition Info:

- Info280 cal., 17g fat (5g sag. fat), 20mg chol, 390mg sod., 24g carb (15g sugars, 7g fiber), 13g pro.

Herb Garden Lasagnas

Servings:6
Cooking Time: 30 Minutes
Ingredients:

- 2 large eggs
- 1 large egg yolk
- 1/4 cup water
- 1 tablespoon olive oil
- 1/2 teaspoon coarsely ground pepper
- 1/4 teaspoon salt
- 1 1/2 cups all-purpose flour
- 1/2 cup semolina flour
- FILLING
- 1 cup whole-milk ricotta cheese
- 1 large egg white, lightly beaten
- 2 tablespoons shredded carrot
- 1 tablespoon minced fresh basil
- 1 tablespoon thinly sliced green onion
- 1 teaspoon minced fresh mint
- 1/4 teaspoon salt
- 1 cup crumbled queso fresco or feta cheese, divided
- 4 cups chopped tomatoes (about 6 medium), divided

Directions:

1. In a small bowl, whisk the first six ingredients. On a clean work surface, mix all-purpose and semolina flours; form into a mound. Make a large well in the center. Pour egg mixture into well. Using a fork or fingers, gradually mix flour mixture into egg mixture, forming a soft dough (dough will be soft and slightly sticky).
2. Lightly dust work surface with flour; knead dough gently five times. Divide into six portions; cover with plastic wrap. Let rest 30 minutes.
3. In a small bowl, mix the first seven filling ingredients; stir in 1/2 cup queso fresco. Grease six individual 12-oz. au gratin dishes; place on baking sheets. Preheat oven to 350°.
4. Fill a Dutch oven three-fourths full with salted water; bring to a boil. On a floured surface, roll each portion into a 20x4-in. rectangle, dusting dough with additional flour as needed.
5. For each lasagna, add one noodle to boiling water; cook 1-2 minutes or until al dente. Place one-fifth of the noodle in bottom of a prepared dish; top with 1 tablespoon of the ricotta mixture and 2 tablespoons tomato. Fold noodle back to cover filling; repeating three times, topping and folding the noodle each time.
6. Sprinkle lasagnas with remaining queso fresco and tomatoes. Bake, covered, 30-35 minutes or until heated through. If desired, sprinkle lasagnas with additional herbs.

Nutrition Info:

- Info363 cal., 13g fat (6g sat. fat), 135mg chol., 343mg sod., 44g carb. (6g sugars, 3g fiber), 19g pro.

Black Beans With Bell Peppers & Rice

Servings:6
Cooking Time: 30 Minutes
Ingredients:

- 1 tablespoon olive oil
- 1 each medium sweet yellow, orange and red pepper, chopped
- 1 large onion, chopped
- 2 garlic cloves, minced
- 2 cans (15 ounces each) black beans, rinsed and drained
- 1 package (8.8 ounces) ready-to-serve brown rice
- 1 1/2 teaspoons ground cumin
- 1/2 teaspoon dried oregano
- 1 1/2 cups (6 ounces) shredded Mexican cheese blend, divided
- 3 tablespoons minced fresh cilantro

Directions:

1. In a large skillet, heat the oil over medium-high heat. Add peppers, onion and garlic; cook and stir 6-8 minutes or until tender. Add beans, rice, cumin and oregano; heat through.
2. Stir in 1 cup cheese; sprinkle with remaining cheese. Remove from heat. Let stand, covered, 5 minutes or until cheese is melted. Sprinkle with cilantro.

Nutrition Info:

- Info347 cal., 12g fat (6g sat. fat), 25mg chol., 477mg sod., 40g carb. (4g sugars, 8g fiber), 15g pro.

Vegetables, Fruit And Side Dishes Recipes

Greek-style Garlic-lemon Potatoes

Servings:6
Cooking Time:30 Minutes
Ingredients:

- 3 tablespoons extra-virgin olive oil
- 3 Yukon Gold potatoes (about 8 ounces each), peeled and cut lengthwise into 8 wedges
- 1½ tablespoons minced fresh oregano
- 3 garlic cloves, minced
- 2 teaspoons grated lemon zest plus 1½ tablespoons juice
- Salt and pepper
- 1½ tablespoons minced fresh parsley

Directions:

1. Heat 2 tablespoons oil in 12-inch nonstick skillet over medium-high heat until shimmering. Add potatoes cut side down in single layer and cook until golden brown on first side (skillet should sizzle but not smoke), about 6 minutes. Using tongs, flip potatoes onto second cut side and cook until golden brown, about 5 minutes. Reduce heat to medium-low, cover, and cook until potatoes are tender, 8 to 12 minutes.
2. Meanwhile, whisk remaining 1 tablespoon oil, oregano, garlic, lemon zest and juice, ½ teaspoon salt, and ½ teaspoon pepper together in small bowl. When potatoes are tender, gently stir in garlic mixture and cook, uncovered, until fragrant, about 2 minutes. Off heat, gently stir in parsley and season with pepper to taste. Serve.

Nutrition Info:

- Info160 cal., 7g fat (1g sag. fat), 0mg chol, 200mg sod., 21g carb (0g sugars, 2g fiber), 3g pro.

Honey-buttered Acorn Squash

Servings: 4
Cooking Time:7 Minutes
Ingredients:

- 1 1/2-pound acorn squash, quartered and seeded
- 1/3 cup water
- 3 tablespoons trans-fat-free margarine (35% vegetable oil)
- 1 1/2 tablespoons honey
- 1/4 teaspoon ground nutmeg
- 1/8 teaspoon salt

Directions:

1. Pierce the outer skin of the squash in several areas with a fork or the tip of a sharp knife.
2. Place the water in a 9-inch glass pie pan and add the squash, cut side up. Cover with plastic wrap and microwave on HIGH for 7 minutes or until the squash is tender when pierced with a fork.
3. Meanwhile, using a fork, stir the remaining ingredients together in a small bowl until well blended.
4. Place the squash on a serving platter and spoon a heaping tablespoon of the honey mixture on the center of each squash quarter.

Nutrition Info:

- Info90 cal., 4g fat (0g sag. fat), 0mg chol, 140mg sod., 13g carb (6g sugars, 3g fiber), 1g pro.

Braised Fennel With White Wine And Parmesan

Servings:4
Cooking Time:25 Minutes
Ingredients:
- 3 tablespoons extra-virgin olive oil
- 2 fennel bulbs, stalks discarded, bulbs cut vertically into ½-inch-thick slices
- Salt and pepper
- ⅓ cup dry white wine
- ¼ cup grated Parmesan cheese

Directions:
1. Heat 2 tablespoons oil in 12-inch nonstick skillet over medium heat until shimmering. Add fennel and sprinkle with ⅛ teaspoon salt and ⅛ teaspoon pepper. Add wine, cover, and simmer for 15 minutes.
2. Turn slices over and continue to simmer, covered, until fennel is nearly tender, has absorbed most of liquid, and starts to turn golden, about 10 minutes.
3. Turn fennel again and continue to cook until golden on second side, about 4 minutes. Transfer to serving platter, drizzle with remaining 1 tablespoon oil, and sprinkle with Parmesan. Serve.

Nutrition Info:
- Info160 cal., 12g fat (2g sag. fat), 5mg chol, 200mg sod., 9g carb (5g sugars, 4g fiber), 3g pro.

Confetti Corn

Servings:4
Cooking Time: 15 Minutes
Ingredients:
- 1/4 cup chopped carrot
- 1 tablespoon olive oil
- 2 3/4 cups fresh or frozen corn, thawed
- 1/4 cup chopped water chestnuts
- 1/4 cup chopped sweet red pepper

Directions:
1. In a large skillet, saute the carrot in oil until crisp-tender. Stir in the corn, water chestnuts and red pepper; heat until warmed through.

Nutrition Info:
- Info140 cal., 4g fat (1g sat. fat), 0 chol., 7mg sod., 26g carb. (3g sugars, 3g fiber), 4g pro.

Slow-cooked Whole Carrots

Servings:6
Cooking Time:45 Minutes
Ingredients:
- 1 tablespoon extra-virgin olive oil
- ½ teaspoon salt
- 1½ pounds carrots, peeled

Directions:
1. Cut parchment paper into 11-inch circle, then cut 1-inch hole in center, folding paper as needed.
2. Bring 3 cups water, oil, and salt to simmer in 12-inch skillet over high heat. Off heat, add carrots, top with parchment, cover skillet, and let sit for 20 minutes.
3. Uncover, leaving parchment in place, and bring to simmer over high heat. Reduce heat to medium-low and cook until most of water has evaporated and carrots are very tender, about 45 minutes.
4. Discard parchment, increase heat to medium-high, and cook, shaking skillet often, until carrots are lightly glazed and no water remains, 2 to 4 minutes. Serve.

Nutrition Info:
- Info60 cal., 2g fat (0g sag. fat), 0mg chol, 100mg sod., 10g carb (5g sugars, 3g fiber), 1g pro.

Roasted Vegetables With Sage

Servings:8
Cooking Time: 35 Minutes
Ingredients:

- 5 cups cubed peeled butternut squash
- 1/2 pound fingerling potatoes (about 2 cups)
- 1 cup fresh Brussels sprouts, halved
- 1 cup fresh baby carrots
- 3 tablespoons butter
- 1 tablespoon minced fresh sage or 1 teaspoon dried sage leaves
- 1 garlic clove, minced
- 1/2 teaspoon salt

Directions:

1. Preheat oven to 425°. Place vegetables in a large bowl. In a microwave, melt butter; stir in remaining ingredients. Add to vegetables and toss to coat.
2. Transfer to a greased 15x10x1-in. baking pan. Roast 35-45 minutes or until tender, stirring occasionally.

Nutrition Info:

- Info122 cal., 5g fat (3g sat. fat), 11mg chol., 206mg sod., 20g carb. (4g sugars, 3g fiber), 2g pro.

Roasted Cauliflower

Servings:6
Cooking Time:20 Minutes
Ingredients:

- 1 head cauliflower (2 pounds)
- ¼ cup extra-virgin olive oil
- Salt and pepper

Directions:

1. Adjust oven rack to lowest position and heat oven to 475 degrees. Line a rimmed baking sheet with aluminum foil. Trim outer leaves off cauliflower and cut stem flush with bottom of head. Cut head into 8 equal wedges. Place wedges, with either cut side down, on lined baking sheet, drizzle with 2 tablespoons oil, and sprinkle with ¼ teaspoon salt and ⅛ teaspoon pepper. Gently rub oil and seasonings into cauliflower. Gently flip cauliflower and repeat on second cut side with remaining 2 tablespoons oil, ¼ teaspoon salt, and ⅛ teaspoon pepper.
2. Cover baking sheet tightly with foil and roast for 10 minutes. Remove foil and continue to roast until bottoms of cauliflower wedges are golden, 8 to 12 minutes.
3. Remove sheet from oven, carefully flip wedges using spatula, and continue to roast until cauliflower is golden all over, 8 to 12 minutes. Transfer to serving dish, season with pepper to taste, and serve.

Nutrition Info:

- Info120 cal., 10g fat (1g sag. fat), 0mg chol, 240mg sod., 8g carb (3g sugars, 3g fiber), 3g pro.

Squash & Mushroom Medley

Servings:5
Cooking Time: 20 Minutes
Ingredients:

- 1 large yellow summer squash, chopped
- 1 large zucchini, chopped
- 1 medium onion, chopped
- 2 teaspoons butter
- 1 can (7 ounces) mushroom stems and pieces, drained
- 2 garlic cloves, minced
- 1/4 teaspoon salt
- 1/8 teaspoon pepper

Directions:

1. In a large skillet, saute the summer squash, zucchini and onion in butter until tender. Add the mushrooms, garlic, salt and pepper; saute 2-3 minutes longer or until heated through.

Nutrition Info:

- Info58 cal., 2g fat (1g sat. fat), 4mg chol., 283mg sod., 9g carb. (5g sugars, 3g fiber), 3g pro.

Roasted Smashed Potatoes

Servings:6
Cooking Time:60 Minutes
Ingredients:

- 2 pounds small Red Bliss potatoes (about 18), scrubbed
- ¼ cup extra-virgin olive oil
- 1 teaspoon chopped fresh thyme
- 1 teaspoon kosher salt
- ⅛ teaspoon pepper

Directions:

1. Adjust oven racks to top and bottom positions and heat oven to 500 degrees. Arrange potatoes on rimmed baking sheet, pour ¾ cup water into baking sheet, and wrap tightly with aluminum foil. Cook on bottom rack until paring knife or skewer slips in and out of potatoes easily (poke through foil to test), 25 to 30 minutes. Remove foil and cool 10 minutes. If any water remains on baking sheet, blot dry with paper towel.
2. Drizzle 2 tablespoons oil over potatoes and roll to coat. Space potatoes evenly on baking sheet and place second baking sheet on top; press down firmly on baking sheet, flattening potatoes until ⅓ to ½ inch thick. Remove top sheet and sprinkle potatoes evenly with thyme, salt, and pepper. Drizzle evenly with remaining 2 tablespoons oil.
3. Roast potatoes on top rack for 15 minutes. Transfer potatoes to bottom rack and continue to roast until well browned, 20 to 30 minutes longer. Serve immediately.

Nutrition Info:

- Info190 cal., 10g fat (1g sag. fat), 0mg chol, 210mg sod., 24g carb (2g sugars, 3g fiber), 3g pro.

Mashed Cauliflower With Sour Cream

Servings: 4
Cooking Time:10 Minutes
Ingredients:

- 1 cup water
- 1 pound fresh or frozen cauliflower florets
- 1/4 cup fat-free sour cream
- 2 tablespoons no-trans-fat margarine (35% vegetable oil)
- 1/4 teaspoon salt
- 1/4 teaspoon black pepper

Directions:

1. Bring the water to boil in a large saucepan and add the cauliflower. Return to a boil, reduce the heat, cover tightly, and simmer 8 minutes or until tender.
2. Drain the cauliflower well and place it in a blender with the remaining ingredients. Hold the lid down tightly and blend until smooth. You may need to turn off the blender and scrape the mixture off the sides once or twice.

Nutrition Info:

- Info60 cal., 3g fat (0g sag. fat), 0mg chol, 240mg sod., 8g carb (3g sugars, 2g fiber), 3g pro.

Creole-simmered Vegetables

Servings: 4
Cooking Time:24 Minutes
Ingredients:

- 1 (14.5-ounce) can stewed tomatoes with Cajun seasonings
- 2 cups frozen pepper and onion stir-fry
- 3/4 cup thinly sliced celery
- 1 tablespoon no-trans-fat margarine (35% vegetable oil)

Directions:

1. Place all the ingredients except the margarine in a medium saucepan and bring to a boil over high heat. Reduce the heat, cover tightly, and simmer 20 minutes or until the onions are very tender.
2. Increase the heat to high and cook 2 minutes, uncovered, to thicken the vegetables slightly. Remove from the heat and stir in the margarine.

Nutrition Info:

- Info60 cal., 1g fat (0g sag. fat), 0mg chol, 210mg sod., 10g carb (6g sugars, 2g fiber), 2g pro.

Garlicky Braised Kale

Servings:8
Cooking Time:19 Minutes
Ingredients:

- 6 tablespoons extra-virgin olive oil
- 1 large onion, chopped fine
- 10 garlic cloves, minced
- ¼ teaspoon red pepper flakes
- 2 cups unsalted chicken broth
- Salt and pepper
- 4 pounds kale, stemmed and cut into 3-inch pieces
- 1 tablespoon lemon juice, plus extra for seasoning

Directions:

1. Heat 3 tablespoons oil in Dutch oven over medium heat until shimmering. Add onion and cook until softened and lightly browned, 5 to 7 minutes. Stir in garlic and pepper flakes and cook until fragrant, about 1 minute. Stir in broth, 1 cup water, and ½ teaspoon salt and bring to simmer.
2. Add one-third of kale, cover, and cook, stirring occasionally, until wilted, 2 to 4 minutes. Repeat with remaining kale in 2 batches. Continue to cook, covered, until kale is tender, 13 to 15 minutes.
3. Remove lid and increase heat to medium-high. Cook, stirring occasionally, until most liquid has evaporated and greens begin to sizzle, 10 to 12 minutes. Off heat, stir in remaining 3 tablespoons oil and lemon juice. Season with pepper and extra lemon juice to taste. Serve.

Nutrition Info:

- Info190 cal., 12g fat (1g sag. fat), 0mg chol, 240mg sod., 17g carb (5g sugars, 6g fiber), 8g pro.

Golden Zucchini

Servings:8
Cooking Time: 10 Minutes
Ingredients:

- 3 cups shredded zucchini
- 2 large eggs
- 2 garlic cloves, minced
- 3/4 teaspoon salt
- 1/2 teaspoon pepper
- 1/4 teaspoon dried oregano
- 1/2 cup all-purpose flour
- 1/2 cup finely chopped sweet onion
- 1 tablespoon butter
- Marinara sauce, warmed, optional

Directions:

1. Place zucchini in a colander to drain; squeeze well to remove excess liquid. Pat dry.
2. In a large bowl, whisk eggs, garlic, salt, pepper and oregano until blended. Stir in flour just until moistened. Fold in zucchini and onion.
3. Lightly grease a griddle with butter; heat over medium heat. Drop the zucchini mixture by 1/4 cupfuls onto griddle; flatten to 1/2-in. thickness (3-in. diameter). Cook 4-5 minutes on each side or until golden brown. If desired, serve with marinara sauce.

Nutrition Info:

- Info145 cal., 6g fat (3g sat. fat), 101mg chol., 510mg sod., 18g carb. (3g sugars, 2g fiber), 6g pro.

Best Baked Sweet Potatoes

Servings:4
Cooking Time:8minutes
Ingredients:

* 4 (8-ounce) sweet potatoes, unpeeled, each lightly pricked with fork in 3 places

Directions:

1. Adjust oven rack to middle position and heat oven to 425 degrees. Place wire rack in aluminum foil–lined rimmed baking sheet and spray rack with vegetable oil spray. Place potatoes on large plate and microwave until potatoes yield to gentle pressure and reach internal temperature of 200 degrees, 6 to 9 minutes, flipping potatoes every 3 minutes.
2. Transfer potatoes to prepared rack and bake for 1 hour (exteriors of potatoes will be lightly browned and potatoes will feel very soft when squeezed).
3. Slit each potato lengthwise; using clean dish towel, hold ends and squeeze slightly to push flesh up and out. Transfer potatoes to serving dish. Serve.

Nutrition Info:

* Info170 cal., 0g fat (0g sag. fat), 0mg chol, 120mg sod., 40g carb (12g sugars, 7g fiber), 3g pro.

Potatoes, Pasta, And Whole Grains Recipes

Noodles With Mustard Greens And Shiitake-ginger Sauce

Servings:6
Cooking Time:10 Minutes.
Ingredients:

* 8 ounces (⅛-inch-wide) brown rice noodles
* 2 tablespoons toasted sesame oil
* 1 tablespoon canola oil
* 8 ounces shiitake mushrooms, stemmed and sliced thin
* 2 cups water
* ¼ cup mirin
* 3 tablespoons rice vinegar
* 2 tablespoons low-sodium soy sauce
* 1 tablespoon grated fresh ginger
* 2 garlic cloves, minced
* ½ ounce dried shiitake mushrooms, rinsed and minced
* 1 teaspoon Asian chili-garlic sauce
* 1 pound mustard greens, stemmed and chopped into 1-inch pieces
* 4 ounces frozen shelled edamame
* 3 scallions, sliced thin
* 2 teaspoons sesame seeds, toasted
* Pepper

Directions:

1. Bring 3 quarts water to boil in large saucepan. Place noodles in large bowl and pour boiling water over noodles. Stir and let soak until noodles are soft and pliable but not fully tender, about 8 minutes, stirring once halfway through soaking. Drain noodles and rinse under cold running water until water runs clear. Drain noodles well, then toss with 2 teaspoons sesame oil. Portion noodles into 6 individual serving bowls; set aside.
2. Heat canola oil in Dutch oven over medium-high heat until shimmering. Add fresh mushrooms and cook, stirring occasionally, until softened and lightly browned, about 5 minutes. Stir in water, mirin, vinegar, soy sauce, ginger, garlic, dried mushrooms, chili-garlic sauce, and 1 teaspoon sesame oil. Bring to simmer and cook until liquid has reduced by half, 8 to 10 minutes.
3. Stir in mustard greens and edamame, return to simmer, and cook, stirring often, until greens are nearly tender, 5 to 7 minutes.
4. Divide mustard green–mushroom mixture and sauce among noodle bowls. Top with scallions and sesame seeds and drizzle with remaining 1 tablespoon sesame oil. Season with pepper to taste and serve.

Nutrition Info:

* Info290 cal., 9g fat (1g sag. fat), 0mg chol, 250mg sod., 43g carb (7g sugars, 7g fiber), 9g pro.

Penne With Fresh Tomato Sauce, Spinach, And Feta

Servings:4
Cooking Time:10minutes
Ingredients:

- 2 tablespoons extra-virgin olive oil
- 2 garlic cloves, minced
- 3 pounds ripe tomatoes, cored, peeled, seeded, and cut into ½-inch pieces
- 5 ounces (5 cups) baby spinach
- 8 ounces (2¼ cups) 100 percent whole-wheat penne
- Salt and pepper
- 4 ounces feta cheese, crumbled (1 cup)
- 2 tablespoons chopped fresh mint or oregano
- 1 tablespoon lemon juice

Directions:

1. Cook oil and garlic in 12-inch skillet over medium heat, stirring often, until garlic turns golden, about 3 minutes. Stir in tomatoes and cook until they begin to lose their shape, about 8 minutes. Stir in spinach, 1 handful at a time, and cook until spinach is wilted and tomatoes have made chunky sauce, 2 3 minutes.
2. Meanwhile, bring 4 quarts water to boil in large pot. Add pasta and 1 teaspoon salt and cook, stirring often, until al dente. Reserve ½ cup cooking water, then drain pasta and return it to pot.
3. Stir ¾ cup feta, mint, lemon juice, ⅛ teaspoon salt, and ⅛ teaspoon pepper into sauce. Add sauce to pasta and toss to combine. Season with pepper to taste and adjust consistency with reserved cooking water as needed. Sprinkle with remaining ¼ cup feta and serve.

Nutrition Info:

- Info390 cal., 15g fat (5g sag. fat), 25mg chol, 420mg sod., 50g carb (10g sugars, 11g fiber), 15g pro.

Wheat Berry Salad With Roasted Red Pepper, Feta, And Arugula

Servings:6
Cooking Time: 70 Minutes
Ingredients:

- 1 cup wheat berries
- Salt
- 2 tablespoons extra-virgin olive oil
- 2 tablespoons sherry vinegar
- 2 garlic cloves, minced
- ½ teaspoon ground cumin
- ⅛ teaspoon cayenne pepper
- 1 (15-ounce) can no-salt-added chickpeas, rinsed
- ½ cup jarred roasted red peppers, rinsed, patted dry, and chopped
- 2 ounces feta cheese, crumbled (½ cup)
- ¼ cup minced fresh cilantro
- 2 ounces (2 cups) baby arugula, chopped coarse

Directions:

1. Bring 4 quarts water to boil in large pot. Add wheat berries and ½ teaspoon salt and cook until tender with slight chew, 60 to 70 minutes.
2. Whisk oil, vinegar, garlic, cumin, and cayenne together in large bowl. Drain wheat berries, add to bowl with dressing, and gently toss to coat. Let cool slightly, about 15 minutes.
3. Stir in chickpeas, red peppers, feta, and cilantro. Add arugula and gently toss to combine. Serve.

Nutrition Info:

- Info230 cal., 7g fat (2g sag. fat), 10mg chol, 170mg sod., 32g carb (2g sugars, 6g fiber), 8g pro.

Fusilli With Zucchini, Tomatoes, And Pine Nuts

Servings:6
Cooking Time:30 Minutes

Ingredients:

- 2 pounds zucchini and/or summer squash, halved lengthwise and sliced ½ inch thick
- Kosher salt and pepper
- 3 tablespoons extra-virgin olive oil
- 3 garlic cloves, minced
- ⅛–½ teaspoon red pepper flakes
- 12 ounces (4½ cups) 100 percent whole-wheat fusilli
- 12 ounces grape tomatoes, halved
- ½ cup chopped fresh basil
- 2 tablespoons balsamic vinegar
- ¼ cup grated Parmesan cheese
- ¼ cup pine nuts, toasted

Directions:

1. Toss squash with 1 tablespoon salt in colander and let drain for 30 minutes. Pat squash dry with paper towels and carefully wipe away any residual salt.
2. Heat ½ tablespoon oil in 12-inch nonstick skillet over high heat until just smoking. Add half of squash and cook, turning once, until golden brown and slightly charred, 5 to 7 minutes, reducing heat if squash begins to scorch; transfer to large plate. Repeat with ½ tablespoon oil and remaining squash; transfer to plate.
3. Heat 1 tablespoon oil in now-empty skillet over medium heat until shimmering. Add garlic and pepper flakes and cook until fragrant, about 30 seconds. Stir in squash and cook until heated through, about 30 seconds.
4. Meanwhile, bring 4 quarts water to boil in large pot. Add pasta and 2 teaspoons salt and cook, stirring often, until al dente. Reserve ½ cup cooking water, then drain pasta and return it to pot. Add squash mixture, tomatoes, basil, vinegar, and remaining 1 tablespoon oil and toss to combine. Adjust consistency with reserved cooking water as needed. Sprinkle individual portions with Parmesan and pine nuts.

Nutrition Info:

- Info340 cal., 14g fat (2g sag. fat), 5mg chol, 220mg sod., 44g carb (7g sugars, 8g fiber), 12g pro.

Rosemary Rice With Fresh Spinach Greens

Servings: 4
Cooking Time:11 Minutes

Ingredients:

- 1 1/2 cups water
- 3/4 cup instant brown rice
- 1/8–1/4 teaspoon dried rosemary
- 1 cup packed spinach leaves, coarsely chopped
- 1 tablespoon no-trans-fat margarine (35% vegetable oil)
- 1/4 teaspoon salt

Directions:

1. Bring the water and rice to a boil in a medium saucepan. Add the rice and rosemary, reduce the heat, cover tightly, and simmer 10 minutes.
2. Remove the saucepan from the heat and stir in remaining ingredients. Toss gently, yet thoroughly, until the spinach has wilted.

Nutrition Info:

- Info140 cal., 2g fat (0g sag. fat), 0mg chol, 190mg sod., 27g carb (0g sugars, 2g fiber), 3g pro.

Warm Farro With Fennel And Parmesan

Servings:6
Cooking Time:30 Minutes
Ingredients:

- 1½ cups whole farro
- Salt and pepper
- 3 tablespoons extra-virgin olive oil
- 1 onion, chopped fine
- 1 small fennel bulb, stalks discarded, bulb halved, cored, and chopped fine
- 3 garlic cloves, minced
- 1 teaspoon minced fresh thyme or ¼ teaspoon dried
- 1 ounce Parmesan cheese, grated (½ cup)
- ¼ cup minced fresh parsley
- 2 teaspoons sherry vinegar, plus extra for seasoning

Directions:

1. Bring 4 quarts water to boil in large pot. Add farro and 1 teaspoon salt and cook until grains are tender with slight chew, 15 to 30 minutes. Drain farro, return to now-empty pot, and cover to keep warm.
2. Heat 2 tablespoons oil in 12-inch skillet over medium heat until shimmering. Add onion, fennel, and ¼ teaspoon salt and cook until softened, 6 to 8 minutes. Stir in garlic and thyme and cook until fragrant, about 30 seconds. Add farro and remaining 1 tablespoon oil and cook until heated through, about 2 minutes. Off heat, stir in Parmesan, parsley, and vinegar. Season with pepper and extra vinegar to taste. Serve.

Nutrition Info:

- Info280 cal., 10g fat (1g sag. fat), 5mg chol, 240mg sod., 41g carb (4g sugars, 6g fiber), 9g pro.

Roasted Sweet Potatoes With Cinnamon

Servings: 4
Cooking Time:15 Minutes
Ingredients:

- 1 pound sweet potatoes, peeled and cut into 3/4-inch pieces
- 1 tablespoon canola oil
- 1 tablespoon sugar
- 1/2 teaspoon ground cinnamon
- 1/8 teaspoon salt

Directions:

1. Preheat the oven to 425°F.
2. Arrange the potatoes on a baking pan lined with a foil. Drizzle the oil over the potatoes and toss to coat completely. Bake 10 minutes, then shake pan to stir. Bake another 5 minutes or until the potatoes are tender when pierced with a fork.
3. Meanwhile, stir the remaining ingredients together in a small bowl.
4. Remove the pan from the oven and sprinkle the potatoes with the cinnamon mixture. Lift up the ends of the foil and fold them over the potatoes, sealing the ends tightly but not pressing down on the potatoes. Let the potatoes stand 15 minutes to develop flavors and release moisture.

Nutrition Info:

- Info110 cal., 3g fat (0g sag. fat), 0mg chol, 95mg sod., 18g carb (8g sugars, 2g fiber), 1g pro.

North African–style Chickpea Salad

Servings:6
Cooking Time:10 Minutes
Ingredients:
- 2 tablespoons extra-virgin olive oil
- 1½ tablespoons lemon juice
- 1 small garlic clove, minced
- ½ teaspoon ground cumin
- ½ teaspoon paprika
- Salt and pepper
- 2 (15-ounce) cans no-salt-added chickpeas, rinsed
- 1 carrot, peeled and shredded
- ½ cup raisins
- 2 tablespoons minced fresh mint

Directions:
1. Whisk oil, lemon juice, garlic, cumin, paprika, and ½ teaspoon salt together in large bowl. Add chickpeas, carrot, raisins, and mint and gently toss to combine. Season with pepper to taste and serve.

Nutrition Info:
- Info190 cal., 5g fat (0g sag. fat), 0mg chol, 230mg sod., 27g carb (11g sugars, 4g fiber), 6g pro.

Spiced Basmati Rice With Cauliflower And Pomegranate

Servings:6
Cooking Time:30minutes
Ingredients:
- ½ head cauliflower (1 pound), cored and cut into ¾-inch florets
- 2 tablespoons extra-virgin olive oil
- Salt and pepper
- ¼ teaspoon ground cumin
- ½ onion, chopped coarse
- ¾ cup basmati rice, rinsed
- 2 garlic cloves, minced
- ¼ teaspoon ground cinnamon
- ¼ teaspoon ground turmeric
- 1¼ cups water
- ¼ cup pomegranate seeds
- 1 tablespoon chopped fresh cilantro
- 1 tablespoon chopped fresh mint

Directions:
1. Adjust oven rack to lowest position and heat oven to 475 degrees. Toss cauliflower with 1 tablespoon oil, ⅛ teaspoon salt, ¼ teaspoon pepper, and ⅛ teaspoon cumin. Arrange cauliflower in single layer on rimmed baking sheet and roast until just tender, 8 to 10 minutes; set aside.
2. Heat remaining 1 tablespoon oil in large saucepan over medium heat until shimmering. Add onion and ¼ teaspoon salt and cook until softened and lightly browned, 5 to 7 minutes. Add rice, garlic, cinnamon, turmeric, and remaining ⅛ teaspoon cumin and cook, stirring frequently, until grain edges begin to turn translucent, about 3 minutes.
3. Stir in water and bring to simmer. Reduce heat to low, cover, and simmer gently until rice is tender and water is absorbed, 16 to 18 minutes.
4. Off heat, lay clean dish towel underneath lid and let pilaf sit for 10 minutes. Add cauliflower to pilaf and fluff gently with fork to combine. Season with pepper to taste. Transfer to serving platter and sprinkle with pomegranate seeds, cilantro, and mint. Serve.

Nutrition Info:
- Info150 cal., 5g fat (1g sag. fat), 0mg chol, 170mg sod., 23g carb (3g sugars, 3g fiber), 3g pro.

Orecchiette With Broccoli Rabe And Sausage

Servings:6
Cooking Time: 7 Minutes
Ingredients:

- ¼ cup extra-virgin olive oil
- 8 ounces sweet Italian chicken sausage, casings removed
- 6 garlic cloves, minced
- ¼ teaspoon red pepper flakes
- 1 pound broccoli rabe, trimmed and cut into 1½-inch pieces
- Salt and pepper
- 12 ounces (3¾ cups) 100 percent whole-wheat orecchiette
- 1 ounce Parmesan or Asiago cheese, grated (½ cup)

Directions:

1. Heat oil in 12-inch nonstick skillet over medium heat until shimmering. Add sausage, breaking up pieces with wooden spoon, and cook until lightly browned, 5 to 7 minutes. Stir in garlic and pepper flakes and cook until fragrant, about 30 seconds; set skillet aside.

2. Meanwhile, bring 4 quarts water to boil in large pot. Add broccoli rabe and 1 teaspoon salt and cook, stirring often, until crisp-tender, about 2 minutes. Using slotted spoon, transfer broccoli rabe to skillet with sausage.

3. Return water to boil, add pasta, and cook, stirring often, until al dente. Reserve 1 cup cooking water, then drain pasta and return it to pot. Add sausage–broccoli rabe mixture, Parmesan, ⅓ cup reserved cooking water, and ¼ teaspoon salt and toss to combine. Season with pepper to taste and adjust consistency with remaining ⅔ cup reserved cooking water as needed. Serve.

Nutrition Info:

- Info380 cal., 16g fat (3g sag. fat), 15mg chol, 490mg sod., 46g carb (2g sugars, 7g fiber), 19g pro.

Parmesan Potato Bake

Servings: 6
Cooking Time:1 Hour
Ingredients:

- 1 1/2 pounds red potatoes, scrubbed and very thinly sliced
- 1/2 cup finely chopped onion
- 3 tablespoons no-trans-fat margarine (35% vegetable oil; divided use)
- 1/8 teaspoon black pepper (divided use)
- 3 tablespoons grated Parmesan cheese (divided use)
- 1/4 teaspoon salt (divided use)

Directions:

1. Preheat the oven to 375°F.

2. Coat a 9-inch deep-dish pie pan with nonstick cooking spray. Put half the potatoes in the pan, then all of the onions, then half of the remaining ingredients. Place the remaining potatoes on top, add the remaining margarine, and sprinkle with the remaining pepper. Cover with foil and bake 45 minutes.

3. Uncover the potatoes and sprinkle with the remaining Parmesan cheese and salt. Bake uncovered for 15 minutes or until the potatoes are tender when pierced with a fork. Let stand 10 minutes to develop flavors.

Nutrition Info:

- Info120 cal., 3g fat (0g sag. fat), 0mg chol, 190mg sod., 20g carb (2g sugars, 2g fiber), 3g pro.

Farro Salad With Cucumber, Yogurt, And Mint

Servings:8
Cooking Time: 30 Minutes
Ingredients:

- 1½ cups whole farro
- Salt and pepper
- 3 tablespoons extra-virgin olive oil
- 2 tablespoons lemon juice
- 2 tablespoons minced shallot
- 2 tablespoons plain 2 percent Greek yogurt
- 1 English cucumber, halved lengthwise, seeded, and cut into ¼-inch pieces
- 6 ounces cherry tomatoes, halved
- 1 cup baby arugula
- 3 tablespoons chopped fresh mint

Directions:
1. Bring 4 quarts water to boil in large pot. Add farro and 1 teaspoon salt and cook until grains are tender with slight chew, 15 to 30 minutes. Drain farro well. Transfer to parchment paper–lined rimmed baking sheet and spread into even layer. Let cool completely, about 15 minutes.
2. Whisk oil, lemon juice, shallot, yogurt, ¼ teaspoon salt, and ¼ teaspoon pepper together in large bowl. Add farro, cucumber, tomatoes, arugula, and mint and gently toss to combine. Season with pepper to taste. Serve.

Nutrition Info:
- Info190 cal., 7g fat (1g sag. fat), 0mg chol, 100mg sod., 30g carb (3g sugars, 4g fiber), 5g pro.

Couscous With Saffron, Raisins, And Toasted Almonds

Servings:6
Cooking Time:12 Minutes
Ingredients:

- 1 cup whole-wheat couscous
- 2 tablespoons extra-virgin olive oil
- 1 onion, chopped fine
- Salt and pepper
- ⅛ teaspoon saffron threads, crumbled
- ⅛ teaspoon ground cinnamon
- ⅛ teaspoon cayenne pepper
- ¾ cup water
- ¾ cup unsalted chicken broth
- ½ cup raisins
- ¼ cup sliced almonds, toasted
- 1½ teaspoons lemon juice

Directions:
1. Toast couscous in medium saucepan over medium-high heat, stirring often, until a few grains begin to brown, about 3 minutes. Transfer couscous to large bowl and set aside.
2. Heat 1 tablespoon oil in now-empty saucepan over medium heat until shimmering. Add onion and ½ teaspoon salt and cook until softened, about 5 minutes. Stir in saffron, cinnamon, and cayenne and cook until fragrant, about 30 seconds. Stir in water, broth, and raisins and bring to boil.
3. Once boiling, immediately pour broth mixture over couscous, cover tightly with plastic wrap, and let sit until grains are tender, about 12 minutes.
4. Add remaining 1 tablespoon oil, almonds, and lemon juice and fluff gently with fork to combine. Season with pepper to taste and serve.

Nutrition Info:
- Info230 cal., 7g fat (1g sag. fat), 0mg chol, 220mg sod., 36g carb (14g sugars, 5g fiber), 6g pro.

Penne With Chicken And Pan-roasted Broccoli

Servings:6
Cooking Time:20 Minutes
Ingredients:

- 2 tablespoons extra-virgin olive oil
- 1 pound broccoli, florets cut into 1½-inch pieces, stems trimmed, peeled, and cut on bias into ¼-inch-thick slices about 1½ inches long
- 8 garlic cloves, peeled (4 sliced thin, 4 minced)
- 1 tablespoon grated lemon zest
- ⅛–¼ teaspoon red pepper flakes
- Salt and pepper
- 3 tablespoons water
- 1 pound boneless, skinless chicken breasts, trimmed of all visible fat and cut into 1-inch pieces
- 3 shallots, minced
- 2 teaspoons minced fresh thyme
- 2 tablespoons all-purpose flour
- 2 cups unsalted chicken broth
- 1 cup dry white wine
- 12 ounces (3½ cups) 100 percent whole-wheat penne
- 1 ounce Parmesan cheese, grated (½ cup)
- 2 tablespoons minced fresh parsley

Directions:

1. Heat 1 tablespoon oil in 12-inch nonstick skillet over medium-high heat until just smoking. Add broccoli stems in even layer and cook, without stirring, until browned on bottoms, about 2 minutes. Add florets to skillet and toss to combine; cook, without stirring, until bottom sides of florets just begin to brown, 1 to 2 minutes longer.
2. Stir in sliced garlic, 1 teaspoon lemon zest, pepper flakes, and ¼ teaspoon pepper and cook until fragrant, about 30 seconds. Stir in water and cover skillet; cook until broccoli is bright green but still crisp, about 2 minutes. Uncover and continue to cook until water has evaporated and broccoli is crisp-tender, about 2 minutes. Transfer broccoli to medium bowl and set aside.
3. Heat remaining 1 tablespoon oil in now-empty skillet over high heat until just smoking. Add chicken and ¼ teaspoon salt and cook, stirring occasionally, until lightly browned but not fully cooked, about 3 minutes; transfer to separate bowl.
4. Reduce heat to medium, add shallots and ⅛ teaspoon salt to now-empty skillet, and cook until just softened, 2 to 3 minutes. Stir in minced garlic and thyme and cook until fragrant, about 30 seconds.
5. Stir in flour and cook for 1 minute. Slowly whisk in broth and wine and bring to simmer, scraping up any browned bits. Cook, stirring occasionally, until sauce has thickened, about 12 minutes. Return chicken and any accumulated juices to skillet. Cook until chicken is cooked through, about 1 minute. Off heat, stir in remaining 2 teaspoons lemon zest.
6. Meanwhile, bring 4 quarts water to boil in large pot. Add pasta and 1 teaspoon salt and cook, stirring often, until al dente. Reserve ½ cup of cooking water, drain pasta, then return to pot. Add chicken-sauce mixture, broccoli, Parmesan, and parsley and toss to combine. Adjust consistency with reserved cooking water as needed. Serve.

Nutrition Info:

- Info420 cal., 10g fat (2g sag. fat), 60mg chol, 400mg sod., 47g carb (4g sugars, 9g fiber), 30g pro.

Slow Cooker Favorites Recipes

Carne Guisada

Servings:12
Cooking Time: 7 Hours
Ingredients:

- 1 bottle (12 ounces) beer
- 1/4 cup all-purpose flour
- 2 tablespoons tomato paste
- 1 jalapeno pepper, seeded and chopped
- 4 teaspoons Worcestershire sauce
- 1 bay leaf
- 2 to 3 teaspoons crushed red pepper flakes
- 2 teaspoons chili powder
- 1 1/2 teaspoons ground cumin
- 1/2 teaspoon salt
- 1/2 teaspoon paprika
- 2 garlic cloves, minced
- 1/2 teaspoon red wine vinegar
- Dash liquid smoke, optional
- 1 boneless pork shoulder butt roast (3 pounds), cut into 2-inch pieces
- 2 large unpeeled red potatoes, chopped
- 1 medium onion, chopped
- Whole wheat tortillas or hot cooked brown rice, lime wedges and chopped fresh cilantro, optional

Directions:

1. In a 4- or 5-qt. slow cooker, mix first 13 ingredients and, if desired, the liquid smoke. Stir in pork, potatoes and onion. Cook mixture, covered, on low until pork is tender, 7-9 hours.
2. Discard bay leaf; skim fat from cooking juices. Shred pork slightly with two forks. Serve pork with the optional remaining ingredients as desired.

Nutrition Info:

- Info261 cal., 12g fat (4g sat. fat), 67mg chol., 200mg sod., 16g carb. (3g sugars, 2g fiber), 21g pro.

Turkey Chili

Servings:8
Cooking Time:4hours
Ingredients:

- 2 pounds ground turkey
- 2 tablespoons water
- Salt and pepper
- ½ teaspoon baking soda
- ¼ cup canola oil
- 3 onions, chopped fine
- 1 red bell pepper, stemmed, seeded, and chopped
- ¼ cup no-salt-added tomato paste
- 3 tablespoons chili powder
- 6 garlic cloves, minced
- 1 tablespoon ground cumin
- ¾ teaspoon dried oregano
- 1¼ cups unsalted chicken broth, plus extra as needed
- 2 tablespoons low-sodium soy sauce
- 2 (15-ounce) cans no-salt-added kidney beans, rinsed
- 1 (28-ounce) can no-salt-added diced tomatoes, drained
- 1 (15-ounce) can no-salt-added tomato sauce
- 2 teaspoons minced canned chipotle chile in adobo sauce
- ¼ cup chopped fresh cilantro
- Lime wedges

Directions:

1. Toss turkey with water, ¼ teaspoon salt, and baking soda in bowl until thoroughly combined. Set aside for 20 minutes.
2. Heat oil in 12-inch skillet over medium heat until shimmering. Add onions and bell pepper and cook until softened and lightly browned, 8 to 10 minutes. Stir in tomato paste, chili powder, garlic, cumin, and oregano and cook until fragrant, about 1 minute.
3. Add half of turkey mixture and cook, breaking up turkey with wooden spoon, until no longer pink, about 5 minutes. Repeat with remaining turkey mixture. Stir in broth and soy sauce, scraping up any browned bits; transfer to slow cooker.
4. Stir beans, tomatoes, tomato sauce, and chipotle into slow cooker. Cover and cook until turkey is tender, 4 to 5 hours on low. Break up any remaining large pieces of turkey with spoon. Adjust consistency with extra hot broth as needed. Season with pepper to taste. Sprinkle individual portions with cilantro and serve with lime wedges.

Nutrition Info:

- Info320 cal., 9g fat (2g sag. fat), 45mg chol, 500mg sod., 25g carb (8g sugars, 10g fiber), 36g pro.

Italian Meatball And Escarole Soup

Servings:6
Cooking Time:5 Hours
Ingredients:

- 2 slices 100 percent whole-wheat sandwich bread, torn into quarters
- ¼ cup 1 percent low-fat milk
- 1 ounce Parmesan cheese, grated (½ cup)
- 3 tablespoons minced fresh parsley
- 1 large egg yolk
- 1½ teaspoons minced fresh oregano or ½ teaspoon dried
- 4 garlic cloves, minced
- Salt and pepper
- 1 pound ground turkey
- 2 teaspoons canola oil
- 1 onion, chopped fine
- ¼ teaspoon red pepper flakes
- 6 cups unsalted chicken broth
- 1 (15-ounce) can no-salt-added cannellini beans, rinsed
- 1 head escarole (1 pound), trimmed and sliced 1 inch thick
- 1 tablespoon lemon juice

Directions:

1. Mash bread, milk, Parmesan, parsley, egg yolk, oregano, half of garlic, and ½ teaspoon pepper into paste in large bowl using fork. Add ground turkey and hand-knead until well combined. Pinch off and roll turkey mixture into tablespoon-size meatballs (about 24 meatballs).

2. Heat 1 teaspoon oil in 12-inch nonstick skillet over medium heat until shimmering. Brown half of meatballs on all sides, about 5 minutes; transfer to slow cooker. Repeat with remaining 1 teaspoon oil and remaining meatballs; transfer to slow cooker.

3. Add onion and ½ teaspoon salt to fat left in skillet and cook over medium heat until onion is softened, about 5 minutes. Stir in pepper flakes and remaining garlic and cook until fragrant, about 30 seconds; transfer to slow cooker. Gently stir in broth and beans, cover, and cook until meatballs are tender, 4 to 6 hours on low or 3 to 5 hours on high.

4. Stir escarole into soup, 1 handful at a time, cover, and cook on high until tender, 15 to 20 minutes. Stir in lemon juice and season with pepper to taste. Serve.

Nutrition Info:

- Info250 cal., 6g fat (2g sag. fat), 65mg chol, 540mg sod., 14g carb (5g sugars, 7g fiber), 30g pro.

Braised Swiss Chard With Shiitakes And Peanuts

Servings:6
Cooking Time: 2 Hours
Ingredients:

- 2 pounds Swiss chard, stems chopped fine, leaves cut into 1-inch pieces
- 4 ounces shiitake mushrooms, stemmed and sliced ¼ inch thick
- 3 garlic cloves, minced
- 2 teaspoons toasted sesame oil
- 2 teaspoons grated fresh ginger
- ⅛ teaspoon red pepper flakes
- 1 tablespoon rice vinegar
- Pepper
- ¼ cup chopped dry-roasted peanuts
- 2 scallions, sliced thin

Directions:

1. Lightly coat slow cooker with vegetable oil spray. Microwave chard stems, mushrooms, garlic, 1 teaspoon oil, 1 teaspoon ginger, and pepper flakes in bowl, stirring occasionally, until vegetables are softened, about 5 minutes; transfer to prepared slow cooker. Stir in chard leaves, cover, and cook until chard is tender, 1 to 2 hours on high.

2. Stir in vinegar, remaining 1 teaspoon oil, and remaining 1 teaspoon ginger. Season with pepper to taste. (Swiss chard can be held on warm or low setting for up to 2 hours.) Sprinkle with peanuts and scallions before serving.

Nutrition Info:

- Info90 cal., 5g fat (1g sag. fat), 0mg chol, 330mg sod., 9g carb (3g sugars, 3g fiber), 5g pro.

Shredded Beef Tacos With Cabbage-carrot Slaw

Servings:6
Cooking Time:4 Hours
Ingredients:

- ½ onion, chopped fine
- 1 ounce (2 to 3) dried ancho chiles, stemmed, seeded, and torn into 1-inch pieces (½ cup)
- 3 garlic cloves, minced
- 1 tablespoon no-salt-added tomato paste
- 1 tablespoon canola oil
- 1 teaspoon minced canned chipotle chile in adobo sauce
- ½ teaspoon ground cinnamon
- ¾ cup water, plus extra as needed
- Salt
- 2 pounds boneless beef chuck-eye roast, trimmed of all visible fat and cut into 1½-inch pieces
- ½ head napa cabbage, cored and sliced thin (6 cups)
- 1 carrot, peeled and shredded
- 1 jalapeño chile, stemmed, seeded, and sliced thin
- ¼ cup lime juice (2 limes), plus lime wedges for serving
- ¼ cup chopped fresh cilantro
- 12 (6-inch) corn tortillas, warmed
- 1 ounce queso fresco, crumbled (¼ cup)

Directions:
1. Microwave onion, anchos, garlic, tomato paste, oil, chipotle, and cinnamon in bowl, stirring occasionally, until onion is softened, about 5 minutes; transfer to slow cooker. Stir in water and ½ teaspoon salt. Stir beef into slow cooker. Cover and cook until beef is tender, 7 to 8 hours on low or 4 to 5 hours on high.
2. Combine cabbage, carrot, jalapeño, lime juice, cilantro, and ¼ teaspoon salt in large bowl. Cover slaw and refrigerate until ready to serve.
3. Using slotted spoon, transfer beef to another large bowl. Using 2 forks, shred beef into bite-size pieces; cover to keep warm.
4. Process cooking liquid in blender until smooth, about 1 minute. Adjust sauce consistency with hot water as needed. Toss beef with 1 cup sauce. Toss slaw to recombine. Divide beef evenly among tortillas and top with slaw and queso fresco. Serve, passing lime wedges and remaining sauce separately.

Nutrition Info:
- Info420 cal., 14g fat (3g sag. fat), 100mg chol, 500mg sod., 36g carb (6g sugars, 7g fiber), 39g pro.

Big-batch Brown Rice With Parmesan And Herbs

Servings:12
Cooking Time:3 Hours
Ingredients:

- 3 cups boiling water
- 2 cups long-grain brown rice, rinsed
- 1 tablespoon unsalted butter
- Salt and pepper
- 2 ounces Parmesan cheese, grated (1 cup)
- ½ cup chopped fresh basil, dill, or parsley
- 2 teaspoons lemon juice

Directions:
1. Lightly coat oval slow cooker with vegetable oil spray. Combine boiling water, rice, butter, ½ teaspoon salt, and ½ teaspoon pepper in prepared slow cooker. Gently press 16 by 12-inch sheet of parchment paper onto surface of water, folding down edges as needed. Cover and cook until rice is tender and all water is absorbed, 2 to 3 hours on high.
2. Discard parchment. Fluff rice with fork, then gently fold in Parmesan, basil, and lemon juice. Season with pepper to taste. Serve.

Nutrition Info:
- Info130 cal., 4g fat (1g sag. fat), 5mg chol, 180mg sod., 24g carb (0g sugars, 2g fiber), 4g pro.

Beef And Garden Vegetable Soup

Servings:6
Cooking Time: 5 Minutes
Ingredients:

- 2 onions, chopped fine
- 3 tablespoons no-salt-added tomato paste
- 4 garlic cloves, minced
- 1 tablespoon minced fresh thyme or 1 teaspoon dried
- ¼ ounce dried porcini mushrooms, rinsed and minced
- 1 tablespoon canola oil
- Salt and pepper
- 6 cups unsalted chicken broth
- 4 carrots, peeled and cut into ½-inch pieces
- 1 (14.5-ounce) can no-salt-added diced tomatoes
- 2 teaspoons low-sodium soy sauce
- 2 pounds beef blade steaks, ¾ to 1 inch thick, trimmed of all visible fat and gristle
- 8 ounces green beans, trimmed and cut on bias into 1-inch lengths
- ¼ cup chopped fresh basil

Directions:

1. Microwave onions, tomato paste, garlic, thyme, porcini, oil, and ½ teaspoon salt in bowl, stirring occasionally, until onions are softened, about 5 minutes; transfer to slow cooker. Stir in broth, carrots, tomatoes and their juice, and soy sauce. Nestle steaks into slow cooker. Cover and cook until beef is tender, 9 to 10 hours on low or 6 to 7 hours on high.
2. Transfer steaks to cutting board, let cool slightly, then shred into bite-size pieces using 2 forks; discard gristle.
3. Microwave green beans with 1 tablespoon water in covered bowl, stirring occasionally, until crisp-tender, 4 to 6 minutes. Drain green beans, then stir into soup along with beef; let sit until heated through, about 5 minutes. Stir in basil and season with pepper to taste. Serve.

Nutrition Info:

- Info330 cal., 12g fat (4g sag. fat), 105mg chol, 560mg sod., 19g carb (10g sugars, 6g fiber), 38g pro.

Turkey Stuffed Peppers

Servings:6
Cooking Time: 4 Hours
Ingredients:

- 2 medium sweet yellow or orange peppers
- 2 medium sweet red peppers
- 2 medium green peppers
- 1 pound lean ground turkey
- 1 small red onion, finely chopped
- 1 small zucchini, shredded
- 2 cups cooked brown rice
- 1 jar (16 ounces) spaghetti sauce, divided
- 1 tablespoon Creole seasoning
- 1/4 teaspoon pepper
- 2 tablespoons shredded Parmesan cheese

Directions:

1. Cut tops from peppers and remove the seeds. Finely chop enough tops to measure 1 cup for filling.
2. In a large skillet, cook turkey, onion and reserved chopped peppers over medium heat for 6-8 minutes or until turkey is no longer pink and vegetables are tender, breaking up turkey into crumbles; drain.
3. Stir in the zucchini; cook and stir about 2 minutes longer. Add the rice, 2/3 cup of the spaghetti sauce, Creole seasoning and pepper.
4. Spread 1/2 cup spaghetti sauce onto the bottom of a greased 6-qt. slow cooker. Fill peppers with turkey mixture; place over sauce. Pour the remaining spaghetti sauce over peppers; sprinkle with cheese.
5. Cook, covered, on low 4-5 hours or until peppers are tender and filling is heated through.

Nutrition Info:

- Info290 cal., 10g fat (3g sat. fat), 63mg chol., 818mg sod., 31g carb. (9g sugars, 5g fiber), 19g pro.

Beets With Oranges And Walnuts

Servings:4
Cooking Time:7hours
Ingredients:

- 1½ pounds beets, trimmed
- 2 oranges
- ¼ cup white wine vinegar
- 1½ tablespoons extra-virgin olive oil
- Salt and pepper
- ¼ cup walnuts, toasted and chopped coarse
- 2 tablespoons minced fresh chives

Directions:

1. Wrap beets individually in aluminum foil and place in oval slow cooker. Add ½ cup water, cover, and cook until beets are tender, 6 to 7 hours on low or 4 to 5 hours on high.
2. Transfer beets to cutting board and carefully remove foil (watch for steam). When beets are cool enough to handle, rub off skins with paper towels and cut into ½-inch-thick wedges.
3. Cut away peel and pith from oranges. Quarter oranges and slice crosswise into ½-inch-thick pieces. Whisk vinegar, oil, ¼ teaspoon salt, and ¼ teaspoon pepper together in large bowl. Add beets and orange pieces and toss to coat. Season with pepper to taste. Sprinkle with walnuts and chives and serve.

Nutrition Info:

- Info190 cal., 10g fat (1g sag. fat), 0mg chol, 260mg sod., 25g carb (18g sugars, 7g fiber), 4g pro.

Herbed Chicken With Warm Bulgur Salad And Yogurt Sauce

Servings:4
Cooking Time:3 Hours
Ingredients:

- 1 cup medium-grind bulgur, rinsed
- 1 cup unsalted chicken broth
- Salt and pepper
- ¼ cup extra-virgin olive oil
- 4 teaspoons minced fresh oregano
- 1¼ teaspoons grated lemon zest plus 2 tablespoons juice
- 1 garlic clove, minced
- Salt and pepper
- ⅛ teaspoon ground cardamom
- 2 (12-ounce) bone-in split chicken breasts, skin removed, trimmed of all visible fat, and halved crosswise
- ½ cup 2 percent Greek yogurt
- ½ cup minced fresh parsley
- 3 tablespoons water
- 8 ounces cherry tomatoes, quartered
- 1 carrot, peeled and shredded
- ¼ cup chopped toasted pistachios

Directions:

1. Lightly coat oval slow cooker with vegetable oil spray. Combine bulgur, broth, and ⅛ teaspoon salt in prepared slow cooker. Microwave 1 tablespoon oil, 1 tablespoon oregano, 1 teaspoon lemon zest, garlic, ¼ teaspoon salt, ¼ teaspoon pepper, and cardamom in bowl until fragrant, about 30 seconds; let cool slightly. Rub chicken with oregano mixture, then arrange, skinned side up, in even layer in prepared slow cooker. Cover and cook until chicken registers 160 degrees, 2 to 3 hours on low.
2. Whisk yogurt, 1 tablespoon parsley, water, remaining 1 teaspoon oregano, remaining ¼ teaspoon lemon zest, and ⅛ teaspoon salt together in bowl. Season sauce with pepper to taste.
3. Transfer chicken to serving platter, brushing any bulgur that sticks to breasts back into slow cooker. Drain bulgur mixture, if necessary, and return to now-empty slow cooker. Add remaining 3 tablespoons oil, remaining 7 tablespoons parsley, lemon juice, tomatoes, carrot, and ⅛ teaspoon salt and fluff with fork to combine. Season with pepper to taste. Sprinkle bulgur salad with pistachios. Serve chicken with salad and yogurt sauce.

Nutrition Info:

- Info500 cal., 23g fat (4g sag. fat), 100mg chol, 440mg sod., 36g carb (5g sugars, 7g fiber), 41g pro.

Lentil Pumpkin Soup

Servings:6
Cooking Time: 7 Hours
Ingredients:

- 1 pound red potatoes (about 4 medium), cut into 1-inch pieces
- 1 can (15 ounces) solid-pack pumpkin
- 1 cup dried lentils, rinsed
- 1 medium onion, chopped
- 3 garlic cloves, minced
- 1/2 teaspoon ground ginger
- 1/2 teaspoon pepper
- 1/8 teaspoon salt
- 2 cans (14 1/2 ounces each) vegetable broth
- 1 1/2 cups water
- Minced fresh cilantro, optional

Directions:
1.   In a 3- or 4-qt. slow cooker, combine first 10 ingredients. Cook, covered, on low 7-9 hours or until potatoes and lentils are tender. If desired, sprinkle servings with cilantro.

Nutrition Info:

- Info210 cal., 1g fat (0 sat. fat), 0 chol., 463mg sod., 42g carb. (5g sugars, 7g fiber), 11g pro.

Slow-cooked Peach Salsa

Servings:11
Cooking Time: 3 Hours
Ingredients:

- 4 pounds tomatoes (about 12 medium), chopped
- 1 medium onion, chopped
- 4 jalapeno peppers, seeded and finely chopped
- 1/2 to 2/3 cup packed brown sugar
- 1/4 cup minced fresh cilantro
- 4 garlic cloves, minced
- 1 teaspoon salt
- 4 cups chopped peeled fresh peaches (about 4 medium), divided
- 1 can (6 ounces) tomato paste

Directions:
1.   In a 5-qt. slow cooker, combine the first seven ingredients; stir in 2 cups peaches. Cook, covered, on low for 3-4 hours or until onion is tender.
2.   Stir tomato paste and remaining peaches into the slow cooker. Cool. Transfer to covered containers. (If freezing, use freezer-safe containers and fill containers to within 1/2 in. of tops.) Refrigerate up to 1 week or freeze up to 12 months. Thaw frozen salsa in refrigerator before serving.

Nutrition Info:

- Info28 cal., 0 fat (0 sat. fat), 0 chol., 59mg sod., 7g carb. (5g sugars, 1g fiber), 1g pro.

Italian Cabbage Soup

Servings:8
Cooking Time: 6 Hours
Ingredients:

- 4 cups chicken stock
- 1 can (6 ounces) tomato paste
- 1 small head cabbage (about 1 1/2 pounds), shredded
- 4 celery ribs, chopped
- 2 large carrots, chopped
- 1 small onion, chopped
- 1 can (15 1/2 ounces) great northern beans, rinsed and drained
- 2 garlic cloves, minced
- 2 fresh thyme sprigs
- 1 bay leaf
- 1/2 teaspoon salt
- Shredded Parmesan cheese, optional

Directions:
1. In a 5- or 6-qt. slow cooker, whisk together stock and tomato paste. Stir in the vegetables, beans, garlic and seasonings. Cook, covered, on low until vegetables are tender, 6-8 hours.
2. Remove thyme sprigs and bay leaf. If desired, serve with cheese.

Nutrition Info:
- Info111 cal., 0 fat (0 sat. fat), 0 chol., 537mg sod., 21g carb. (7g sugars, 6g fiber), 8g pro.

Teriyaki Beef Stew

Servings:8
Cooking Time: 6 1/2 Hours
Ingredients:

- 2 pounds beef stew meat
- 1 bottle (12 ounces) ginger beer or ginger ale
- 1/4 cup teriyaki sauce
- 2 garlic cloves, minced
- 2 tablespoons sesame seeds
- 2 tablespoons cornstarch
- 2 tablespoons cold water
- 2 cups frozen peas, thawed
- Hot cooked rice, optional

Directions:
1. In a nonstick skillet, brown beef in batches. Transfer to a 3-qt. slow cooker.
2. In a small bowl, combine the ginger beer, teriyaki sauce, garlic and sesame seeds; pour over beef. Cover and cook on low for 6-8 hours or until the meat is tender.
3. Combine cornstarch and cold water until smooth; gradually stir into stew. Stir in peas. Cover and cook on high for 30 minutes or until thickened. Serve with rice if desired.

Nutrition Info:
- Info310 cal., 12g fat (4g sat. fat), 94mg chol., 528mg sod., 17g carb. (9g sugars, 2g fiber), 33g pro.

Special Treats Recipes

Dark Chocolate Bark With Pepitas And Goji Berries

Servings:16
Cooking Time: 30 Minutes
Ingredients:
- 1 pound 70 percent dark chocolate, 12 ounces chopped fine, 4 ounces grated
- 2 teaspoons ground cinnamon
- 1 teaspoon chipotle chile powder
- 2 cups roasted pepitas, 1¾ cups left whole, ¼ cup chopped
- 1 cup dried goji berries, chopped
- 1 teaspoon coarse sea salt

Directions:
1. Make parchment paper sling for 13 by 9-inch baking pan by folding 2 long sheets of parchment; first sheet should be 13 inches wide and second sheet should be 9 inches wide. Lay sheets in pan perpendicular to each other, with extra parchment hanging over edges of pan. Push parchment into corners and up sides of pan, smoothing parchment flush to pan.
2. Microwave 12 ounces finely chopped chocolate in large bowl at 50 percent power, stirring every 15 seconds, until melted but not much hotter than body temperature (check by holding in the palm of your hand), 2 to 3 minutes. Stir in 4 ounces grated chocolate, cinnamon, and chile powder until smooth and chocolate is completely melted (returning to microwave for no more than 5 seconds at a time to finish melting if necessary).
3. Stir 1¾ cups whole pepitas and ¾ cup goji berries into chocolate mixture. Working quickly, use rubber spatula to spread chocolate mixture evenly into prepared pan. Sprinkle with remaining ¼ cup chopped pepitas and remaining ¼ cup goji berries and gently press topping into chocolate. Sprinkle evenly with salt and refrigerate until chocolate is set, about 30 minutes.
4. Using parchment overhang, lift chocolate out of pan and transfer to cutting board; discard parchment. Using serrated knife and gentle sawing motion, cut chocolate into 16 even pieces. Serve.

Nutrition Info:
- Info260 cal., 21g fat (9g sag. fat), 0mg chol, 140mg sod., 20g carb (10g sugars, 4g fiber), 8g pro.

Pomegranate And Nut Chocolate Clusters

Servings:12
Cooking Time: 30 Minutes
Ingredients:
- ⅓ cup pecans, toasted and chopped
- ¼ cup shelled pistachios, toasted and chopped
- 2 tablespoons unsweetened flaked coconut, toasted
- 2 tablespoons pomegranate seeds
- 3 ounces semisweet chocolate, chopped fine

Directions:
1. Line rimmed baking sheet with parchment paper. Combine pecans, pistachios, coconut, and pomegranate seeds in bowl.
2. Microwave 2 ounces chocolate in bowl at 50 percent power, stirring often, until about two-thirds melted, 45 to 60 seconds. Remove bowl from microwave; stir in remaining 1 ounce chocolate until melted. If necessary, microwave chocolate at 50 percent power for 5 seconds at a time until melted.
3. Working quickly, measure 1 teaspoon melted chocolate onto prepared sheet and spread into 2½-inch wide circle using back of spoon. Repeat with remaining chocolate, spacing circles 1½ inches apart.
4. Sprinkle pecan mixture evenly over chocolate and press gently to adhere. Refrigerate until chocolate is firm, about 30 minutes. Serve.

Nutrition Info:
- Info80 cal., 6g fat (2g sag. fat), 0mg chol, 0mg sod., 6g carb (5g sugars, 1g fiber), 1g pro.

Banana-pineapple Cream Pies

Servings:2
Cooking Time: 15 Minutes
Ingredients:

- 1/4 cup cornstarch
- 1/4 cup sugar
- 1 can (20 ounces) unsweetened crushed pineapple, undrained
- 3 medium bananas, sliced
- Two 9-inch graham cracker crusts (about 6 ounces each)
- 1 carton (8 ounces) frozen whipped topping, thawed

Directions:

1. In a large saucepan, combine cornstarch and sugar. Stir in pineapple until blended. Bring to a boil; cook and stir 1-2 minutes or until thickened.
2. Arrange bananas over bottom of each crust; spread the pineapple mixture over tops. Refrigerate at least 1 hour before serving. Top with the whipped topping.

Nutrition Info:

- Info205 cal., 8g fat (3g sat. fat), 0 chol., 122mg sod., 33g carb. (23g sugars, 1g fiber), 1g pro.

Oatmeal Cookies With Chocolate And Goji Berries

Servings:24
Cooking Time:10 Minutes
Ingredients:

- 1 cup (5 ounces) all-purpose flour
- ¾ teaspoon salt
- ½ teaspoon baking soda
- 1 cup packed (7 ounces) dark brown sugar
- ⅔ cup canola oil
- 1 tablespoon water
- 1 teaspoon vanilla extract
- 1 large egg plus 1 large yolk
- 3 cups (9 ounces) old-fashioned rolled oats
- 1 cup dried goji berries
- 3½ ounces 70 percent dark chocolate, chopped into ¼-inch pieces

Directions:

1. Adjust oven rack to middle position and heat oven to 375 degrees. Line 2 rimmed baking sheets with parchment paper. Whisk flour, salt, and baking soda together in bowl; set aside.
2. Whisk sugar, oil, water, and vanilla together in large bowl until well combined. Add egg and yolk and whisk until smooth. Using rubber spatula, stir in flour mixture until fully combined. Add oats, goji berries, and chocolate and stir until evenly distributed (mixture will be stiff).
3. Divide dough into 24 portions, each about heaping 2 tablespoons. Using damp hands, tightly roll into balls and space 2 inches apart on prepared sheets, 12 balls per sheet. Press balls to ¾-inch thickness.
4. Bake, 1 sheet at a time, until edges are set and centers are soft but not wet, 8 to 10 minutes, rotating sheet halfway through baking. Let cookies cool on sheets for 5 minutes, then transfer to wire rack. Let cookies cool completely before serving.

Nutrition Info:

- Info190 cal., 9g fat (2g sag. fat), 15mg chol, 100mg sod., 24g carb (11g sugars, 2g fiber), 3g pro.

Pineapple Breeze Torte

Servings:12
Cooking Time: 5 Minutes
Ingredients:

- 3 packages (3 ounces each) soft ladyfingers, split
- FILLING
- 1 package (8 ounces) fat-free cream cheese
- 3 ounces cream cheese, softened
- 1/3 cup sugar
- 2 teaspoons vanilla extract
- 1 carton (8 ounces) frozen reduced-fat whipped topping, thawed
- TOPPING
- 1/3 cup sugar
- 3 tablespoons cornstarch
- 1 can (20 ounces) unsweetened crushed pineapple, undrained

Directions:

1. Line bottom and sides of an ungreased 9-in. springform pan with ladyfinger halves; reserve remaining ladyfingers for layering.
2. Beat cream cheeses, sugar and vanilla until smooth; fold in whipped topping. Spread half of the mixture over bottom ladyfingers. Layer with the remaining ladyfingers, overlapping as needed. Spread with the remaining filling. Refrigerate, covered, while preparing topping.
3. In a small saucepan, mix sugar and cornstarch; stir in pineapple. Bring to a boil over medium heat, stirring constantly; cook and stir until thickened, 1-2 minutes. Cool the mixture completely.
4. Spread topping gently over torte. Refrigerate, covered, until set, at least 4 hours. Remove rim from pan.

Nutrition Info:

- Info243 cal., 7g fat (5g sat. fat), 87mg chol., 156mg sod., 39g carb. (27g sugars, 1g fiber), 6g pro.

Nectarines And Berries In Prosecco

Servings:8
Cooking Time:15 Minutes
Ingredients:

- 10 ounces (2 cups) blackberries or raspberries
- 10 ounces strawberries, hulled and quartered (2 cups)
- 1 pound nectarines, pitted and cut into ¼-inch wedges
- 1 tablespoon sugar
- 1 tablespoon orange liqueur, such as Grand Marnier or triple sec
- 2 tablespoons chopped fresh mint
- ¼ teaspoon grated lemon zest
- ¾ cup chilled prosecco

Directions:

1. Gently toss blackberries, strawberries, nectarines, sugar, orange liqueur, mint, and lemon zest together in large bowl. Let sit at room temperature, stirring occasionally, until fruit begins to release its juices, about 15 minutes. Just before serving, pour prosecco over fruit.

Nutrition Info:

- Info80 cal., 0g fat (0g sag. fat), 0mg chol, 0mg sod., 14g carb (10g sugars, 3g fiber), 1g pro.

Whole-wheat Blueberry Muffins

Servings:12
Cooking Time:18 Minutes

Ingredients:

- 1 cup sliced almonds, lightly toasted
- 1 cup (5½ ounces) whole-wheat flour
- ¾ cup (3¾ ounces) all-purpose flour
- 2 teaspoons baking powder
- ½ teaspoon baking soda
- ¾ teaspoon salt
- 1 cup low-fat buttermilk
- ⅔ cup packed (4⅔ ounces) dark brown sugar
- 2 large eggs
- ¼ cup canola oil
- 2 teaspoons vanilla extract
- 7½ ounces (1½ cups) fresh or frozen blueberries

Directions:

1. Adjust oven rack to middle position and heat oven to 400 degrees. Spray 12-cup muffin tin, including top, generously with canola oil spray. Pulse ¼ cup almonds in food processor until coarsely chopped, 4 to 6 pulses; transfer to small bowl and set aside for topping.

2. Add whole-wheat flour, all-purpose flour, baking powder, baking soda, salt, and remaining ¾ cup almonds to now-empty processor and process until well combined and almonds are finely ground, about 30 seconds; transfer to large bowl.

3. In separate bowl, whisk buttermilk, sugar, eggs, oil, and vanilla until combined. Using rubber spatula, stir buttermilk mixture into almond-flour mixture until just combined (do not overmix). Gently fold in blueberries until incorporated.

4. Divide batter evenly among prepared muffin cups (cups will be filled to rim) and sprinkle with reserved chopped almonds. Bake until golden brown and toothpick inserted in center comes out with few crumbs attached, 16 to 18 minutes, rotating tin halfway through baking.

5. Let muffins cool in tin on wire rack for 10 minutes. Remove muffins from tin and let cool for 20 minutes before serving.

Nutrition Info:

- Info240 cal., 10g fat (1g sag. fat), 30mg chol, 310mg sod., 32g carb (14g sugars, 3g fiber), 6g pro.

Peanut Butter Snack Bars

Servings:3
Cooking Time: 25 Minutes

Ingredients:

- 3 1/4 cups Kashi Heart to Heart honey toasted oat cereal
- 2 3/4 cups old-fashioned oats
- 1 cup unblanched almonds
- 1/2 cup sunflower kernels
- 1/4 cup ground flaxseed
- 1/4 cup uncooked oat bran cereal
- 1/4 cup wheat bran
- 1/4 cup whole flaxseed
- 3 tablespoons sesame seeds
- 2 cups creamy peanut butter
- 1 1/2 cups honey
- 1 teaspoon vanilla extract

Directions:

1. In a large bowl, combine the first nine ingredients. In a small saucepan, combine peanut butter and honey. Cook over medium heat until peanut butter is melted, stirring occasionally. Remove from the heat. Stir in vanilla. Pour over cereal mixture; mix well.

2. Transfer to a greased 15x10x1-in. baking pan; gently press into pan. Cool completely. Cut into bars. Store in an airtight container.

Nutrition Info:

- Info215 cal., 12g fat (2g sat. fat), 0 chol., 87mg sod., 24g carb. (14g sugars, 3g fiber), 7g pro.

Holiday Cookies

Servings:2
Cooking Time:20 Minutes

Ingredients:

- COOKIES
- 6 tablespoons (2⅔ ounces) granulated sugar
- 2½ cups (12½ ounces) all-purpose flour
- ⅛ teaspoon salt
- 16 tablespoons unsalted butter, cut into 16 pieces and softened
- 1 ounce cream cheese, softened
- 2 teaspoons vanilla extract
- GLAZE
- 1 ounce cream cheese
- 1–2 tablespoons 1 percent low-fat milk
- ⅛ teaspoon salt
- ¾ cup (3 ounces) confectioners' sugar

Directions:

1. FOR THE COOKIES Using stand mixer fitted with paddle, mix sugar, flour, and salt together on low speed until combined, about 1 minute. Add butter, 1 piece at a time, and mix until only pea-size pieces remain, about 1 minute. Add cream cheese and vanilla and mix until dough just begins to form large clumps, about 30 seconds.

2. Transfer dough to clean counter, knead until dough forms cohesive mass, then divide into 2 equal pieces. Shape each piece into 4-inch disk, then wrap in plastic wrap and refrigerate until firm, at least 30 minutes or up to 3 days.

3. Adjust oven rack to middle position and heat oven to 375 degrees. Working with 1 piece of dough at a time, roll ⅛ inch thick between 2 sheets of parchment paper. Slide dough, still between parchment, onto baking sheet and refrigerate until firm, about 20 minutes.

4. Line 2 baking sheets with parchment. Working with 1 sheet of dough at a time, remove top sheet of parchment and cut dough as desired using cookie cutters; space cookies ¾ inch apart on prepared sheets. (Dough scraps can be patted together, chilled, and rerolled once.)

5. Bake cookies, 1 sheet at a time, until lightly puffed but still underdone, about 5 minutes. Remove partially baked cookies from oven and, holding sheet firmly with both hands, rap pan flat against open oven door 3 to 5 times until puffed cookies flatten. Rotate pan, return cookies to oven, and continue to bake until light golden brown around edges, 4 to 6 minutes. Let cookies cool completely on sheet.

6. FOR THE GLAZE Whisk cream cheese, 1 tablespoon milk, and salt together in medium bowl until smooth. Whisk in confectioners' sugar until smooth, adding remaining 1 tablespoon milk as needed until glaze is thin enough to drizzle. Drizzle or decorate each cookie with glaze as desired. Let glaze set for at least 6 hours before serving.

Nutrition Info:

- Info90 cal., 5g fat (3g sag. fat), 15mg chol, 20mg sod., 11g carb (4g sugars, 0g fiber), 1g pro.

Strawberry Pot Stickers

Servings:32
Cooking Time: 10 Minutes
Ingredients:

- 3 ounces milk chocolate, chopped
- 1/4 cup half-and-half cream
- 1 teaspoon butter
- 1 teaspoon vanilla extract
- 1/4 teaspoon ground cinnamon
- POT STICKERS
- 2 cups chopped fresh strawberries
- 3 ounces milk chocolate, chopped
- 1 tablespoon brown sugar
- 1/4 teaspoon ground cinnamon
- 32 pot sticker or gyoza wrappers
- 1 large egg, lightly beaten
- 2 tablespoons canola oil, divided
- 1/2 cup water, divided

Directions:

1. Place chocolate in a small bowl. In a small saucepan, bring cream and butter just to a boil. Pour over chocolate; whisk until smooth. Stir in vanilla and cinnamon. Cool to room temperature, stirring occasionally.

2. For pot stickers, in a small bowl, toss strawberries and chopped chocolate with brown sugar and cinnamon. Place 1 tablespoon mixture in center of 1 gyoza wrapper. (Cover remaining wrappers with a damp paper towel until ready to use.)

3. Moisten wrapper edge with egg. Fold wrapper over filling; seal edges, pleating the front side several times to form a pleated pouch. Repeat with remaining wrappers and filling. Stand pot stickers on a work surface to flatten bottoms; curve slightly to form crescent shapes, if desired.

4. In a large skillet, heat 1 tablespoon oil over medium-high heat. Arrange half of the pot stickers, flat side down, in concentric circles in pan; cook 1-2 minutes or until bottoms are golden brown. Add 1/4 cup water; bring to a simmer. Cook, covered, 3-5 minutes or until water is almost absorbed and wrappers are tender.

5. Cook, uncovered, 1 minute or until bottoms are crisp and the water is completely evaporated. Repeat with remaining pot stickers. Serve the pot stickers with chocolate sauce.

Nutrition Info:

- Info58 cal., 3g fat (1g sat. fat), 6mg chol., 18mg sod., 8g carb. (4g sugars, 0 fiber), 1g pro.

Baked Elephant Ears

Servings:2
Cooking Time: 10 Minutes
Ingredients:

- 1 package (1/4 ounce) active dry yeast
- 1/4 cup warm water (110° to 115°)
- 2 cups all-purpose flour
- 4 1/2 teaspoons sugar
- 1/2 teaspoon salt
- 1/3 cup cold butter, cubed
- 1/3 cup fat-free milk
- 1 large egg yolk
- FILLING
- 2 tablespoons butter, softened
- 1/2 cup sugar
- 2 teaspoons ground cinnamon
- CINNAMON SUGAR
- 1/2 cup sugar
- 3/4 teaspoon ground cinnamon

Directions:

1. In a small bowl, dissolve yeast in warm water. In a large bowl, mix flour, sugar and salt; cut in butter until crumbly. Stir milk and egg yolk into yeast mixture; add to flour mixture, stirring to form a stiff dough (dough will be sticky). Cover with plastic wrap and refrigerate 2 hours.

2. Preheat oven to 375°. Turn dough onto a lightly floured surface; roll dough into an 18x10-in. rectangle. Spread with softened butter to within 1/4 in. of edges. Mix sugar and cinnamon; sprinkle over butter. Roll up jelly-roll style, starting with a long side; pinch seam to seal. Cut crosswise into 24 slices. Cover slices with plastic wrap until ready to flatten.

3. In a small bowl, mix ingredients for cinnamon sugar. Place a 6-in.-square piece of waxed paper on a work surface; sprinkle with 1/2 teaspoon cinnamon sugar. Top with one slice of dough; sprinkle dough with an additional 1/2 teaspoon cinnamon sugar. Roll dough to a 4-in. circle. Using waxed paper, flip dough onto a baking sheet coated with cooking spray. Repeat with remaining ingredients, placing slices 2 in. apart. Bake 7-9 minutes or until golden brown. Cool on wire racks.

Nutrition Info:

- Info109 cal., 4g fat (2g sat. fat), 18mg chol., 76mg sod., 18g carb. (9g sugars, 0 fiber), 1g pro.

Buttermilk Peach Ice Cream

Servings:2
Cooking Time: 15 Minutes
Ingredients:

- 2 pounds ripe peaches (about 7 medium), peeled and quartered
- 1/2 cup sugar
- 1/2 cup packed brown sugar
- 1 tablespoon lemon juice
- 1 teaspoon vanilla extract
- Pinch salt
- 2 cups buttermilk
- 1 cup heavy whipping cream

Directions:

1. Place peaches in a food processor; process until smooth. Add sugars, lemon juice, vanilla and salt; process until blended.
2. In a bowl, mix buttermilk and cream. Stir in the peach mixture. Refrigerate, covered, 1 hour or until cold.
3. Fill cylinder of ice cream maker no more than two-thirds full. Freeze according to manufacturer's directions, refrigerating any remaining mixture to process later. Transfer ice cream to freezer containers, allowing headspace for expansion. Freeze 2-4 hours or until firm. Let ice cream stand at room temperature 10 minutes before serving.

Nutrition Info:

- Info137 cal., 6g fat (4g sat. fat), 22mg chol., 75mg sod., 20g carb. (19g sugars, 1g fiber), 2g pro.

Roasted Plums With Dried Cherries And Almonds

Servings:8
Cooking Time: 10 Minutes
Ingredients:

- 2 tablespoons unsalted butter
- 4 ripe but firm plums (4 to 6 ounces each), peeled, halved, and cored
- 1¼ cups dry white wine
- ½ cup dried unsweetened tart cherries
- 3 tablespoons sugar
- ¼ teaspoon ground cinnamon
- ⅛ teaspoon salt
- 1 teaspoon lemon juice
- ⅓ cup sliced almonds, toasted

Directions:

1. Adjust oven rack to middle position and heat oven to 450 degrees. Melt butter in 12-inch ovensafe skillet over medium-high heat. Place plum halves cut side down in skillet and cook, without moving them, until just beginning to brown, 3 to 5 minutes.
2. Transfer skillet to oven and roast plums for 5 minutes. Using tongs, carefully flip plums and continue to roast until tip of paring knife easily pierces fruit, about 5 minutes.
3. Carefully remove skillet from oven (skillet handle will be hot) and transfer plums to platter. Add wine, cherries, sugar, cinnamon, and salt to now-empty skillet and bring to simmer over medium-high heat. Cook, whisking to scrape up any browned bits, until sauce is reduced and has consistency of maple syrup, 7 to 10 minutes.
4. Off heat, stir in lemon juice. Pour sauce over plums and sprinkle with almonds. Serve.

Nutrition Info:

- Info150 cal., 5g fat (2g sag. fat), 10mg chol, 40mg sod., 19g carb (14g sugars, 2g fiber), 1g pro.

Gran's Apple Cake

Servings:18
Cooking Time: 35 Minutes

Ingredients:

- 1 2/3 cups sugar
- 2 large eggs
- 1/2 cup unsweetened applesauce
- 2 tablespoons canola oil
- 2 teaspoons vanilla extract
- 2 cups all-purpose flour
- 2 teaspoons baking soda
- 2 teaspoons ground cinnamon
- 3/4 teaspoon salt
- 6 cups chopped peeled tart apples
- 1/2 cup chopped pecans
- FROSTING
- 4 ounces reduced-fat cream cheese
- 2 tablespoons butter, softened
- 1 teaspoon vanilla extract
- 1 cup confectioners' sugar

Directions:

1. Preheat oven to 350°. Coat a 13x9-in. baking pan with cooking spray.

2. In a large bowl, beat sugar, eggs, applesauce, oil and vanilla until well blended. In another bowl, whisk flour, baking soda, cinnamon and salt; gradually beat into sugar mixture. Fold in apples and pecans.

3. Transfer to prepared pan. Bake 35-40 minutes or until top is golden brown and a toothpick inserted in center comes out clean. Cool completely in pan on a wire rack.

4. In a small bowl, beat cream cheese, butter and vanilla until smooth. Gradually beat in confectioners' sugar (mixture will be soft). Spread over cake. Refrigerate leftovers.

Nutrition Info:

- Info241 cal., 7g fat (2g sat. fat), 29mg chol., 284mg sod., 42g carb. (30g sugars, 1g fiber), 3g pro.

Salads Recipes

Artichoke Tomato Toss

Servings: 4
Cooking Time: 4 Minutes
Ingredients:

- 1/2 of a 14-ounce can quartered artichoke hearts, drained
- 1 cup grape tomatoes, halved
- 1 tablespoons fat-free Caesar or Italian dressing
- 1 ounce crumbled, reduced-fat, sun-dried tomato and basil feta cheese
- 2 tablespoons chopped fresh parsley (optional)

Directions:

1. In a medium bowl, toss the artichoke hearts, tomatoes, and dressing gently, yet thoroughly. Add the feta and toss gently again.
2. Serve immediately or cover with plastic wrap and refrigerate up to 3 days.

Nutrition Info:

- Info45 cal., 1g fat (0g sag. fat), 5mg chol, 270mg sod., 6g carb (2g sugars, 3g fiber), 3g pro.

Mediterranean Chopped Salad

Servings:6
Cooking Time: 30 Minutes
Ingredients:

- 12 ounces cherry tomatoes, quartered
- 1 cucumber, peeled, halved lengthwise, seeded, and cut into ½-inch pieces
- Salt and pepper
- 3 tablespoons extra-virgin olive oil
- 3 tablespoons red wine vinegar
- 1 garlic clove, minced
- 1 (15-ounce) can no-salt-added chickpeas, rinsed
- ⅓ cup pitted kalamata olives, chopped
- ¼ cup finely chopped red onion
- 1 romaine lettuce heart (6 ounces), cut into ½-inch pieces
- 3 ounces feta cheese, crumbled (¾ cup)
- ½ cup chopped fresh parsley

Directions:

1. Toss tomatoes and cucumber with ½ teaspoon salt in colander and let drain for 15 to 30 minutes.
2. Whisk oil, vinegar, and garlic together in large bowl. Add tomato mixture, chickpeas, olives, and onion and gently toss to coat. Let sit at room temperature until flavors meld, about 5 minutes.
3. Add lettuce, feta, and parsley and gently toss to coat. Season with pepper to taste. Serve.

Nutrition Info:

- Info180 cal., 10g fat (2g sag. fat), 10mg chol, 330mg sod., 13g carb (3g sugars, 3g fiber), 6g pro.

Seaside Shrimp Salad

Servings: 4
Cooking Time:5 Minutes
Ingredients:

- 1 1/2 pounds peeled raw fresh or frozen and thawed shrimp
- 2 tablespoons reduced-fat mayonnaise
- 1 1/2 teaspoons seafood seasoning
- 6 tablespoons lemon juice

Directions:

1. Bring water to boil in a large saucepan over high heat. Add the shrimp and return to a boil. Reduce the heat and simmer, uncovered, 2–3 minutes or until the shrimp is opaque in the center.
2. Drain the shrimp in a colander, rinse with cold water for 30 seconds, and pat dry with paper towels. Let stand 10 minutes to cool completely.
3. Place shrimp in a medium bowl with the mayonnaise, seafood seasoning, and lemon juice. Stir gently to coat. Cover with plastic wrap and refrigerate 2 hours. Serve as is or over tomato slices or lettuce leaves.

Nutrition Info:

- Info130 cal., 2g fat (0g sag. fat), 205mg chol, 430mg sod., 3g carb (1g sugars, 0g fiber), 26g pro.

Balsamic Three-bean Salad

Servings:12
Cooking Time: 25 Minutes
Ingredients:

- 2 pounds fresh green beans, trimmed and cut into 2-inch pieces
- 1/2 cup balsamic vinaigrette
- 1/4 cup sugar
- 1 garlic clove, minced
- 3/4 teaspoon salt
- 2 cans (16 ounces each) kidney beans, rinsed and drained
- 2 cans (15 ounces each) cannellini beans, rinsed and drained
- 4 fresh basil leaves, torn

Directions:

1. Fill a Dutch oven three-fourths full with water; bring to a boil. Add green beans; cook, uncovered, 3-6 minutes or until crisp-tender. Drain and immediately drop into ice water. Drain and pat dry.
2. In a large bowl, whisk vinaigrette, sugar, garlic and salt until sugar is dissolved. Add canned beans and green beans; toss to coat. Refrigerate, covered, at least 4 hours. Stir in basil just before serving.

Nutrition Info:

- Info190 cal., 3g fat (0 sat. fat), 0 chol., 462mg sod., 33g carb. (8g sugars, 9g fiber), 9g pro.

Parmesan-peppercorn Dressing

Servings:1
Cooking Time: 1 Week
Ingredients:

- This dressing works well with all types of greens.
- 2 tablespoons buttermilk
- 2 tablespoons mayonnaise
- 2 tablespoons low-fat sour cream
- 2 tablespoons grated Parmesan cheese
- 1 tablespoon water
- 1½ teaspoons lemon juice
- ½ teaspoon Dijon mustard
- ½ teaspoon minced shallot
- ¼ teaspoon pepper
- ¼ teaspoon garlic powder

Directions:

1. Whisk lemon zest and juice, mayonnaise, mustard, salt, and pepper together in bowl. While whisking constantly, drizzle in oil until completely emulsified. (Vinaigrette can be refrigerated for up to 1 week; whisk to recombine.)

Nutrition Info:

- Info70 cal., 6g fat (1g sag. fat), 5mg chol, 135mg sod., 1g carb (1g sugars, 0g fiber), 2g pro.

Red, White & Blue Potato Salad

Servings:12
Cooking Time: 10 Minutes
Ingredients:

- 1 1/4 pounds small purple potatoes (about 11), quartered
- 1 pound small Yukon Gold potatoes (about 9), quartered
- 1 pound small red potatoes (about 9), quartered
- 1/2 cup chicken stock
- 1/4 cup white wine or additional chicken stock
- 2 tablespoons sherry vinegar
- 2 tablespoons white wine vinegar
- 1 1/2 teaspoons Dijon mustard
- 1 1/2 teaspoons stone-ground mustard
- 3/4 teaspoon salt
- 1/2 teaspoon coarsely ground pepper
- 6 tablespoons olive oil
- 3 celery ribs, chopped
- 1 small sweet red pepper, chopped
- 8 green onions, chopped
- 3/4 pound bacon strips, cooked and crumbled
- 3 tablespoons each minced fresh basil, dill and parsley
- 2 tablespoons toasted sesame seeds

Directions:

1. Place all potatoes in a Dutch oven; add water to cover. Bring to a boil. Reduce heat; cook, uncovered, 10-15 minutes or until tender. Drain; transfer to a large bowl. Drizzle potatoes with stock and wine; toss gently, allowing liquids to absorb.
2. In a small bowl, whisk vinegars, mustards, salt and pepper. Gradually whisk in oil until blended. Add the vinaigrette, vegetables, bacon and herbs to the potato mixture; toss to combine. Sprinkle with sesame seeds. Serve warm.

Nutrition Info:

- Info221 cal., 12g fat (2g sat. fat), 10mg chol., 405mg sod., 22g carb. (2g sugars, 3g fiber), 7g pro.

Lemon Vinaigrette

Servings:1
Cooking Time:10 Minutes
Ingredients:

- This vinaigrette is best for dressing mild greens.
- ¼ teaspoon grated lemon zest plus 1 tablespoon juice
- ½ teaspoon mayonnaise
- ½ teaspoon Dijon mustard
- ⅛ teaspoon salt
- Pinch pepper
- 3 tablespoons extra-virgin olive oil

Directions:

1. Whisk lemon zest and juice, mayonnaise, mustard, salt, and pepper together in bowl. While whisking constantly, drizzle in oil until completely emulsified. (Vinaigrette can be refrigerated for up to 1 week; whisk to recombine.)

Nutrition Info:

- Info100 cal., 11g fat (1g sag. fat), 0mg chol, 90mg sod., 0g carb (0g sugars, 0g fiber), 0g pro.

Summer Macaroni Salad

Servings:16
Cooking Time: 15 Minutes
Ingredients:
- 1 package (16 ounces) elbow macaroni
- 1 cup reduced-fat mayonnaise
- 3 to 4 tablespoons water or 2% milk
- 2 tablespoons red wine vinegar
- 1 tablespoon sugar
- 1 1/2 teaspoons salt
- 1/4 teaspoon garlic powder
- 1/4 teaspoon pepper
- 1 small sweet yellow, orange or red pepper, finely chopped
- 1 small green pepper, finely chopped
- 1 small onion, finely chopped
- 1 celery rib, finely chopped
- 2 tablespoons minced fresh parsley

Directions:
1. Cook macaroni according to package directions. Drain; rinse with cold water and drain again.
2. In a small bowl, mix mayonnaise, water, vinegar, sugar and seasonings until blended. In a large bowl, combine macaroni, peppers, onion and celery. Add 1 cup dressing; toss gently to coat. Refrigerate, covered, 2 hours or until cold. Cover and refrigerate remaining dressing to add just before serving.
3. To serve, stir in reserved dressing. Sprinkle with parsley.

Nutrition Info:
- Info160 cal., 6g fat (1g sat. fat), 5mg chol., 320mg sod., 24g carb. (3g sugars, 1g fiber), 4g pro.

Pesto Quinoa Salad

Servings:4
Cooking Time: 25 Minutes
Ingredients:
- 2/3 cup water
- 1/3 cup quinoa, rinsed
- 2 tablespoons prepared pesto
- 1 tablespoon finely chopped sweet onion
- 1 tablespoon olive oil
- 1 teaspoon balsamic vinegar
- 1/4 teaspoon salt
- 1 medium sweet red pepper, chopped
- 1 cup cherry tomatoes, quartered
- 2/3 cup fresh mozzarella cheese pearls (about 4 ounces)
- 2 tablespoons minced fresh basil, optional

Directions:
1. In a small saucepan, bring water to a boil; stir in quinoa. Reduce heat; simmer, covered, until the iquid is absorbed, 10-12 minutes. Cool slightly.
2. Mix pesto, onion, oil, vinegar and salt; stir in pepper, tomatoes, cheese and quinoa. Refrigerate, covered, to allow flavors to blend, 1-2 hours. If desired, stir in basil.

Nutrition Info:
- Info183 cal., 11g fat (4g sat. fat), 15mg chol., 268mg sod., 14g carb. (3g sugars, 2g fiber), 6g pro.

Buttermilk Coleslaw

Servings:10
Cooking Time:2hours
Ingredients:

- 1 head red or green cabbage (2 pounds), cored and sliced thin
- Salt and pepper
- 1 cup buttermilk
- ¼ cup mayonnaise
- ¼ cup low-fat sour cream
- 3 scallions, sliced thin
- 3 tablespoons minced fresh parsley or cilantro
- 2 teaspoons cider vinegar, plus extra for seasoning
- 1 teaspoon Dijon mustard
- 2 carrots, peeled and shredded

Directions:

1. Toss cabbage with 1 teaspoon salt in colander and let sit until wilted, about 1 hour. Rinse cabbage under cold water, drain, and thoroughly pat dry with paper towels.

2. Whisk buttermilk, mayonnaise, sour cream, scallions, parsley, vinegar, mustard, ¼ teaspoon salt, and ¼ teaspoon pepper together in large bowl until smooth. Add dried cabbage and carrots and gently toss to coat. Cover and refrigerate until flavors meld, about 1 hour or up to 24 hours. Season with pepper and extra vinegar to taste. Serve.

Nutrition Info:

- Info90 cal., 4g fat (1g sag. fat), 5mg chol, 190mg sod., 9g carb (5g sugars, 3g fiber), 3g pro.

Green Bean & Potato Salad

Servings:10
Cooking Time: 20 Minutes
Ingredients:

- 2 pounds red potatoes (about 6 medium), cubed
- 1 pound fresh green beans, trimmed and halved
- 1 small red onion, halved and thinly sliced
- 1/4 cup chopped fresh mint, optional
- DRESSING
- 1/2 cup canola oil
- 1/4 cup white vinegar
- 2 tablespoons lemon juice
- 1 teaspoon salt
- 1/2 teaspoon garlic powder
- 1/4 teaspoon pepper

Directions:

1. Place cubed potatoes in a 6-qt. stockpot; add water to cover. Bring to a boil. Reduce heat; cook, uncovered, 10-15 minutes or until tender, adding green beans during the last 4 minutes of cooking. Drain.

2. Transfer potatoes and green beans to a large bowl; add onion and, if desired, mint. In a small bowl, whisk dressing ingredients until blended. Pour over potato mixture; toss gently to coat. Refrigerate, covered, at least 2 hours before serving.

Nutrition Info:

- Info183 cal., 11g fat (1g sat. fat), 0 chol., 245mg sod., 19g carb. (2g sugars, 3g fiber), 3g pro.

Watermelon & Spinach Salad

Servings:8
Cooking Time: 30 Minutes
Ingredients:
- 1/4 cup rice vinegar or white wine vinegar
- 1 tablespoon grated lime peel
- 2 tablespoons lime juice
- 2 tablespoons canola oil
- 4 teaspoons minced fresh gingerroot
- 2 garlic cloves, minced
- 1/2 teaspoon salt
- 1/4 teaspoon sugar
- 1/4 teaspoon pepper
- SALAD
- 4 cups fresh baby spinach or arugula
- 3 cups cubed seedless watermelon
- 2 cups cubed cantaloupe
- 2 cups cubed English cucumber
- 1/2 cup chopped fresh cilantro
- 2 green onions, chopped

Directions:
1. In a small bowl, whisk the first nine ingredients. In a large bowl, combine salad ingredients. Drizzle with dressing and toss to coat; serve immediately.

Nutrition Info:
- Info84 cal., 4g fat (0 sat. fat), 0 chol., 288mg sod., 13g carb. (10g sugars, 1g fiber), 1g pro.

Spinach, Apple & Pecan Salad

Servings:16
Cooking Time: 15 Minutes
Ingredients:
- 2 packages (6 ounces each) fresh baby spinach
- 1 medium apple, chopped
- 1 cup (4 ounces) crumbled feta cheese
- 1 cup glazed pecans
- 1/2 cup chopped red onion
- 1/3 cup dried cranberries
- 5 bacon strips, cooked and crumbled, optional
- DRESSING
- 2 tablespoons cider vinegar
- 1 tablespoon sugar
- 1/2 teaspoon Dijon mustard
- 1/8 teaspoon pepper
- 1/4 cup canola oil

Directions:
1. In a large bowl, combine the first six ingredients; stir in bacon if desired.
2. For dressing, in a small bowl, whisk vinegar, sugar, mustard and pepper until blended. Gradually whisk in oil. Pour over salad; toss to coat.

Nutrition Info:
- Info109 cal., 8g fat (1g sat. fat), 4mg chol., 116mg sod., 9g carb. (6g sugars, 1g fiber), 2g pro.

Mediterranean Tuna Salad

Servings:6
Cooking Time:1week
Ingredients:

- 3 tablespoons lemon juice, plus extra for seasoning
- 2 teaspoons Dijon mustard
- Pepper
- 5 tablespoons extra-virgin olive oil
- ¼ cup minced red onion
- 1 garlic clove, minced
- 4 (5-ounce) cans solid white tuna in water, drained and flaked
- 2 celery ribs, minced
- 1 red bell pepper, stemmed, seeded, and chopped fine
- ¼ cup pitted kalamata olives, minced
- ¼ cup minced fresh parsley

Directions:

1. Whisk lemon juice, mustard, and ½ teaspoon pepper in large bowl until combined. While whisking constantly, drizzle in oil until completely emulsified. Stir in red onion and garlic and let sit for 5 minutes. Add tuna, celery, bell pepper, olives, and parsley and gently toss to coat. (Salad can be refrigerated for up to 24 hours.) Season with extra lemon juice and pepper to taste. Serve.

Nutrition Info:

- Info200 cal., 14g fat (2g sag. fat), 25mg chol, 300mg sod., 3g carb (1g sugars, 1g fiber), 15g pro.

Meat Recipes

Egg Roll Noodle Bowl

Servings:4
Cooking Time: 30 Minutes
Ingredients:

- 1 tablespoon sesame oil
- 1/2 pound ground pork
- 1 tablespoon soy sauce
- 1 garlic clove, minced
- 1 teaspoon ground ginger
- 1/2 teaspoon salt
- 1/4 teaspoon ground turmeric
- 1/4 teaspoon pepper
- 6 cups shredded cabbage (about 1 small head)
- 2 large carrots, shredded (about 2 cups)
- 4 ounces rice noodles
- 3 green onions, thinly sliced
- Additional soy sauce, optional

Directions:

1. In a large skillet, heat the oil over medium-high heat; cook and crumble pork until browned, 4-6 minutes. Stir in soy sauce, garlic and seasonings. Add cabbage and carrots; cook 4-6 minutes longer or until vegetables are tender, stirring occasionally.
2. Cook rice noodles according to the package directions; drain and add immediately to pork mixture, tossing to combine. Sprinkle with green onions. If desired, serve with additional soy sauce.

Nutrition Info:

- Info302 cal., 12g fat (4g sat. fat), 38mg chol., 652mg sod., 33g carb. (2g sugars, 4g fiber), 14g pro.

Balsamic Beef Kabob Sandwiches

Servings:8
Cooking Time: 10 Minutes
Ingredients:

- 1/4 cup balsamic vinegar
- 1/4 cup olive oil
- 2 garlic cloves, minced
- 1 teaspoon dried rosemary, crushed
- 1/2 teaspoon pepper, divided
- 1/4 teaspoon salt, divided
- 1 1/2 pounds beef top sirloin steak, cut into 1/4-inch-thick strips
- 2 medium onions
- 8 naan flatbreads
- 2 cups chopped heirloom tomatoes

Directions:

1. Mix first four ingredients; stir in 1/4 teaspoon pepper and 1/8 teaspoon salt. Toss with the beef; let stand for 20 minutes.
2. Cut each onion into eight wedges; thread onto metal or soaked wooden skewers. Thread beef strips, weaving back and forth, onto separate skewers.
3. Grill onions, covered, over medium heat until tender, 5-7 minutes per side. Grill beef, covered, over medium heat until desired doneness, 3-4 minutes per side. Grill the flatbreads until lightly browned, 1-2 minutes per side.
4. Toss tomatoes with the remaining pepper and salt. Remove onion and beef from skewers; serve on flatbreads. Top with tomatoes.

Nutrition Info:

- Info353 cal., 14g fat (3g sat. fat), 39mg chol., 595mg sod., 34g carb. (7g sugars, 2g fiber), 23g pro.

Simply Seared Beef Tenderloin

Servings: 4
Cooking Time:11 Minutes
Ingredients:

- 4 (5-ounce) beef tenderloin steaks, about 3/4-inch thick, trimmed of fat
- 1 large split garlic clove
- 1/4 teaspoon coarsely ground black pepper
- 1/4 teaspoon salt
- 2 teaspoons Worcestershire sauce
- 1/2 teaspoon beef bouillon granules
- 1/2 cup water
- 2 cups cooked wild rice

Directions:

1. Rub the beef with the garlic clove. Place a large nonstick skillet over medium-high heat until hot. Coat the skillet with nonstick cooking spray, add the beef, and cook 3 minutes. Turn and cook another 2 minutes.
2. Reduce the heat to medium low and cook the steaks 4 minutes longer or until they are done as desired, turning once. Set aside on a separate plate.
3. Increase the heat to medium high, add the remaining ingredients, bring to a boil, and continue boiling 1 minute or until the mixture measures 1/4 cup liquid. Pour the juices over the beef. Serve each tenderloin with 1/2 cup wild rice.

Nutrition Info:

- Info260 cal., 8g fat (2g sag. fat), 75mg chol, 340mg sod., 19g carb (1g sugars, 2g fiber), 29g pro.

Braised Lamb With Tomatoes And Red Wine

Servings:6
Cooking Time:20 Minutes
Ingredients:
- 2 pounds boneless lamb leg, trimmed of all visible fat and cut into 1-inch pieces
- Salt and pepper
- 2 tablespoons extra-virgin olive oil
- 1 onion, chopped fine
- 3 garlic cloves, minced
- ¼ teaspoon ground cinnamon
- ½ cup dry red wine
- 1 (28-ounce) can no-salt-added whole peeled tomatoes, drained and chopped
- 2 tablespoons minced fresh parsley

Directions:
1. Adjust oven rack to lower-middle position and heat oven to 300 degrees. Pat lamb dry with paper towels and sprinkle with ½ teaspoon salt and ¼ teaspoon pepper. Heat 1 tablespoon oil in Dutch oven over medium-high heat until just smoking. Brown lamb on all sides, 8 to 10 minutes; transfer to bowl.
2. Add remaining 1 tablespoon oil and onions to fat left in pot and cook over medium heat until onions are softened, about 5 minutes. Stir in garlic and cinnamon and cook until fragrant, about 30 seconds. Stir in wine, scraping up any browned bits, and cook until reduced by half, about 1 minute.
3. Stir in tomatoes and lamb along with any accumulated juices and bring to simmer. Cover, transfer pot to oven, and cook until meat is tender, 1¼ to 1½ hours. Stir in parsley and season with pepper to taste. Serve.

Nutrition Info:
- Info260 cal., 12g fat (3g sag. fat), 85mg chol, 380mg sod., 6g carb (3g sugars, 1g fiber), 29g pro.

Easy Marinated Flank Steak

Servings:8
Cooking Time: 15 Minutes
Ingredients:
- 3 tablespoons ketchup
- 1 tablespoon chopped onion
- 1 tablespoon canola oil
- 1 teaspoon brown sugar
- 1 teaspoon Worcestershire sauce
- 1 garlic clove, minced
- 1/8 teaspoon pepper
- 1 beef flank steak (about 2 pounds)

Directions:
1. In a large resealable plastic bag, combine the first seven ingredients. Add beef; seal bag and turn to coat. Refrigerate 8 hours or overnight.
2. Drain beef, discarding marinade. Lightly coat grill rack with cooking oil.
3. Grill beef, covered, over medium heat or broil 4 in. from heat 6-8 minutes on each side or until meat reaches desired doneness (for medium-rare, a thermometer should read 145°; medium, 160°; well-done, 170°). To serve, thinly slice across the grain.

Nutrition Info:
- Info192 cal., 10g fat (4g sat. fat), 54mg chol., 145mg sod., 2g carb. (2g sugars, 0 fiber), 22g pro.

Pork With Tomato Caper Sauce

Servings: 4
Cooking Time:10 Minutes
Ingredients:
- 2 tablespoons tomato paste with oregano, basil, and garlic
- 2 tablespoons capers, drained and mashed with a fork
- 2/3 cup water, divided use
- 1/8 teaspoon salt
- 4 (4-ounce) boneless pork chops, trimmed of fat

Directions:
1. Using a fork, stir the tomato paste, capers, and 1/3 cup water together in a small bowl.
2. Place a medium nonstick skillet over medium-high heat until hot. Coat the skillet with nonstick cooking spray, add the pork chops, and cook 3 minutes.
3. Turn the pork chops and immediately reduce the heat to medium. Spoon the tomato mixture evenly on top of each pork chop, cover tightly, and cook 5 minutes or until the pork chops are barely pink in the center. The sauce may be dark in some areas.
4. Remove the skillet from the heat and add the remaining 1/3 cup water and salt. Turn the pork chops over several times to remove the sauce. Place the pork chops on a serving plate and set aside.
5. Increase the heat to medium high. Bring the sauce to a boil, stirring constantly, and boil 1 minute or until the sauce begins to thicken slightly and measures 1/2 cup. Spoon the sauce over the pork chops.

Nutrition Info:
- Info140 cal., 3g fat (1g sag. fat), 65mg chol, 330mg sod., 2g carb (1g sugars, 0g fiber), 25g pro.

One-pan Roasted Pork Chops And Vegetables With Parsley Vinaigrette

Servings:4
Cooking Time:30 Seconds
Ingredients:
- 1 pound Yukon Gold potatoes, unpeeled, halved lengthwise and sliced ½ inch thick
- 1 pound carrots, peeled and cut into 3-inch lengths, thick ends quartered lengthwise
- 1 fennel bulb, stalks discarded, bulb halved, cored, and cut into ½-inch-thick wedges
- 10 garlic cloves, peeled
- 3 tablespoons plus 1 teaspoon extra-virgin olive oil
- 2 teaspoons minced fresh rosemary or ¾ teaspoon dried
- Salt and pepper
- 1 teaspoon paprika
- 1 teaspoon ground coriander
- 2 (10-ounce) bone-in center-cut pork chops, 1 inch thick, trimmed of all visible fat
- 4 teaspoons red wine vinegar
- 2 tablespoons minced fresh parsley
- 1 small shallot, minced

Directions:
1. Adjust oven rack to upper-middle position and heat oven to 450 degrees. Toss potatoes, carrots, fennel, garlic, 1 tablespoon oil, rosemary, ¼ teaspoons salt, and ¼ teaspoon pepper together in bowl. Spread vegetables into single layer on rimmed baking sheet. Roast until beginning to soften, about 25 minutes.
2. Combine 1 teaspoon oil, paprika, coriander, ¼ teaspoon salt, and 1 teaspoon pepper in bowl. Pat pork dry with paper towels, then rub with spice mixture. Lay chops on top of vegetables and continue to roast until pork register 145 degrees and vegetables are tender, 10 to 15 minutes, rotating sheet halfway through roasting.
3. Remove sheet from oven, tent with aluminum foil, and let rest for 5 minutes. Whisk remaining 2 tablespoons oil, vinegar, parsley, shallot, ¼ teaspoon salt, and ¼ teaspoon pepper together in bowl. Transfer chops to carving board, carve meat from bone, and slice ½ inch thick. Drizzle vinaigrette over pork before serving with vegetables.

Nutrition Info:
- Info480 cal., 19g fat (4g sag. fat), 80mg chol, 640mg sod., 39g carb (8g sugars, 7g fiber), 36g pro.

Parmesan Pork Chops With Spinach Salad

Servings:4
Cooking Time: 30 Minutes
Ingredients:

- 3 medium tomatoes, seeded and chopped
- 1 tablespoon olive oil
- 1 tablespoon lemon juice
- 1 small garlic clove, minced
- 1/2 teaspoon salt, divided
- 1/4 teaspoon pepper, divided
- 2 large egg whites
- 1 tablespoon Dijon mustard
- 1/2 teaspoon dried oregano
- 1/2 cup dry bread crumbs
- 3 tablespoons grated Parmesan cheese
- 4 thin boneless pork loin chops (1/2 inch thick and 3 ounces each)
- 4 cups fresh baby spinach

Directions:

1. In a large bowl, combine tomatoes, oil, lemon juice, garlic, 1/4 teaspoon salt and 1/8 teaspoon pepper; toss gently to combine.
2. In a shallow bowl, whisk egg whites, mustard, oregano and remaining salt and pepper until blended. In another shallow bowl, mix bread crumbs with cheese. Dip pork chops in egg white mixture, then coat with the bread crumb mixture.
3. Place a large nonstick skillet coated with cooking spray over medium heat. Add pork chops; cook 2-3 minutes on each side or until golden brown and pork is tender.
4. Add spinach to tomato mixture; toss to combine. Serve with pork chops.

Nutrition Info:

- Info223 cal., 10g fat (3g sat. fat), 43mg chol., 444mg sod., 12g carb. (3g sugars, 2g fiber), 22g pro.

Asparagus Beef Stir-fry On Potatoes

Servings:4
Cooking Time: 15 Minutes
Ingredients:

- 2 large baking potatoes (about 12 ounces each)
- 2 tablespoons butter
- 1/4 cup reduced-sodium soy sauce
- 2 teaspoons balsamic vinegar
- 2 teaspoons canola oil, divided
- 1 pound beef top sirloin steak, cut into thin strips
- 1 1/2 cups cut fresh asparagus (1 inch)
- 1 1/2 cups sliced fresh mushrooms
- 1/4 teaspoon salt
- 1/8 teaspoon pepper

Directions:

1. Scrub potatoes; pierce several times with a fork. Place on a microwave-safe plate. Microwave, uncovered, on high until tender, 12-16 minutes, turning once. Cool slightly.
2. In a small saucepan, melt butter over medium heat. Heat until the butter is golden brown, 3-4 minutes, stirring constantly. Remove from heat; stir in soy sauce and vinegar. Keep warm.
3. In a large skillet, heat 1 teaspoon oil over medium-high heat; stir-fry beef until browned, 2-3 minutes. Remove from pan.
4. In same pan, stir-fry asparagus and mushrooms in remaining oil until the asparagus is crisp-tender, 2-3 minutes. Stir in beef, salt and pepper; heat the mixture through.
5. Cut potatoes lengthwise in half; fluff pulp with a fork. Top with beef mixture; drizzle with sauce.

Nutrition Info:

- Info387 cal., 13g fat (6g sat. fat), 61mg chol., 832mg sod., 37g carb. (4g sugars, 5g fiber), 31g pro.

Fried Green Tomato Stacks

Servings:4
Cooking Time: 15 Minutes
Ingredients:

- 1/4 cup fat-free mayonnaise
- 1/4 teaspoon grated lime peel
- 2 tablespoons lime juice
- 1 teaspoon minced fresh thyme or 1/4 teaspoon dried thyme
- 1/2 teaspoon pepper, divided
- 1/4 cup all-purpose flour
- 2 large egg whites, lightly beaten
- 3/4 cup cornmeal
- 1/4 teaspoon salt
- 2 medium green tomatoes
- 2 medium red tomatoes
- 2 tablespoons canola oil
- 8 slices Canadian bacon

Directions:

1. Mix the first four ingredients and 1/4 teaspoon pepper; refrigerate until serving. Place flour in a shallow bowl; place egg whites in a separate shallow bowl. In a third bowl, mix cornmeal, salt and remaining pepper.
2. Cut each tomato crosswise into four slices. Lightly coat each slice in flour; shake off excess. Dip in the egg whites, then in cornmeal mixture.
3. In a large nonstick skillet, heat oil over medium heat. In batches, cook tomatoes until golden brown, about 4-5 minutes per side.
4. In same pan, lightly brown Canadian bacon on both sides. For each serving, stack one slice each green tomato, bacon and red tomato. Serve with the sauce.

Nutrition Info:

- Info284 cal., 10g fat (1g sat. fat), 16mg chol., 679mg sod., 37g carb. (6g sugars, 3g fiber), 12g pro.

Grapefruit-zested Pork

Servings: 4
Cooking Time:6 Minutes
Ingredients:

- 3 tablespoons lite soy sauce
- 1/2–1 teaspoon grapefruit zest
- 3 tablespoons grapefruit juice
- 1 jalapeño pepper, seeded and finely chopped, or 1/8–1/4 teaspoon dried red pepper flakes
- 4 thin lean pork chops with bone in (about 1 1/4 pounds total)

Directions:

1. Combine all ingredients in a large zippered plastic bag. Seal tightly and toss back and forth to coat evenly. Refrigerate overnight or at least 8 hours.
2. Preheat the broiler.
3. Coat the broiler rack and pan with nonstick cooking spray, arrange the pork chops on the rack (discarding the marinade), and broil 2 inches away from the heat source for 3 minutes. Turn and broil 3 minutes longer or until the pork is no longer pink in the center.

Nutrition Info:

- Info130 cal., 3g fat (1g sag. fat), 60mg chol, 270mg sod., 2g carb (1g sugars, 0g fiber), 23g pro.

Tender Green Pepper'd Top Round

Servings: 4
Cooking Time:60 Minutes
Ingredients:

- 1 pound boneless top round steak, trimmed of fat and cut in 4 equal pieces
- 1/4 cup fat-free Italian salad dressing
- 1 cup water
- 1/4 cup ketchup
- 1/4 teaspoon salt
- 1/4 teaspoon black pepper
- 2 medium green bell peppers, cut in thin strips

Directions:

1.   Place the beef and salad dressing in a large zippered plastic bag. Seal tightly and shake back and forth to coat evenly. Refrigerate overnight or at least 8 hours, turning occasionally.

2.   Stir the water, ketchup, salt, and black pepper together in a small bowl and set aside.

3.   Place a large nonstick skillet over medium-high heat until hot. Coat the skillet with nonstick cooking spray. Remove the beef from the marinade, discard the marinade, and place the steaks in the skillet. Cook 3 minutes, then turn and cook another 2 minutes.

4.   Reduce the heat to medium low and cook the steaks 4 minutes longer or until they are done as desired, turning once. Add the green peppers and pour the ketchup mixture over all. Bring to a boil, reduce the heat, cover tightly, and simmer 55 minutes or until very tender.

Nutrition Info:

- Info160 cal., 3g fat (1g sag. fat), 60mg chol, 430mg sod., 8g carb (6g sugars, 1g fiber), 25g pro.

Grilled Flank Steak With Summer Vegetables

Servings:6
Cooking Time:20 Minutes
Ingredients:

- 1 red onion, sliced into ½-inch-thick rounds
- 8 ounces cherry tomatoes
- 2 zucchini, sliced lengthwise into ¾-inch-thick planks
- 1 pound eggplant, sliced lengthwise into ¾-inch-thick planks
- 2 tablespoons extra-virgin olive oil
- Salt and pepper
- 1½ pounds flank steak, trimmed of all visible fat
- Lime wedges

Directions:

1.   Thread onion rounds from side to side onto two 12-inch metal skewers. Thread cherry tomatoes onto two 12-inch metal skewers. Brush onion rounds, tomatoes, zucchini, and eggplant with oil and sprinkle with ½ teaspoon pepper. Pat steak dry with paper towels and sprinkle with ¼ teaspoon salt and ⅛ teaspoon pepper.

2.   FOR A CHARCOAL GRILL Open bottom grill vent completely. Light large chimney starter filled with charcoal briquettes (6 quarts). When top coals are partially covered with ash, pour evenly over grill. Set cooking grate in place, cover, and open lid vent completely. Heat grill until hot, about 5 minutes.

3.   FOR A GAS GRILL Turn all burners to high, cover, and heat grill until hot, about 15 minutes. Leave all burners on high.

4.   Clean and oil cooking grate. Place steak, onion and tomato skewers, zucchini, and eggplant on grill. Cook (covered if using gas), flipping steak and turning vegetables as needed, until steak is well browned and registers 120 to 125 degrees (for medium-rare) and vegetables are slightly charred and tender, 7 to 12 minutes. Transfer steak and vegetables to carving board as they finish grilling and tent with aluminum foil. Let steak rest for 10 minutes.

5.   Meanwhile, using tongs, slide tomatoes and onions off skewers. Cut onion rounds, zucchini, and eggplant into 2- to 3-inch pieces. Arrange vegetables on serving platter and season with pepper to taste. Slice steak thin against grain on bias and arrange on platter with vegetables. Serve with lime wedges.

Nutrition Info:

- Info270 cal., 15g fat (4g sag. fat), 75mg chol, 170mg sod., 10g carb (6g sugars, 3g fiber), 26g pro.

Power Lasagna

Servings:8
Cooking Time: 40 Minutes
Ingredients:

- 9 whole wheat lasagna noodles
- 1 pound lean ground beef (90% lean)
- 1 medium zucchini, finely chopped
- 1 medium onion, finely chopped
- 1 medium green pepper, finely chopped
- 3 garlic cloves, minced
- 1 jar (24 ounces) meatless pasta sauce
- 1 can (14 1/2 ounces) no-salt-added diced tomatoes, drained
- 1/2 cup loosely packed basil leaves, chopped
- 2 tablespoons ground flaxseed
- 5 teaspoons Italian seasoning
- 1/4 teaspoon pepper
- 1 carton (15 ounces) fat-free ricotta cheese
- 1 package (10 ounces) frozen chopped spinach, thawed and squeezed dry
- 1 large egg, lightly beaten
- 2 tablespoons white balsamic vinegar
- 2 cups (8 ounces) shredded part-skim mozzarella cheese
- 1/4 cup grated Parmesan cheese

Directions:

1. Preheat oven to 350°. Cook noodles according to the package directions. Meanwhile, in a 6-qt. stockpot, cook beef, zucchini, onion and green pepper over medium heat until beef is no longer pink, breaking up beef into crumbles. Add garlic; cook 1 minute longer. Drain.
2. Stir in pasta sauce, diced tomatoes, basil, flax, Italian seasoning and pepper; heat though. Drain noodles and rinse in cold water.
3. In a small bowl, mix ricotta cheese, spinach, egg and vinegar. Spread 1 cup meat mixture into a 13x9-in. baking dish coated with cooking spray. Layer with three noodles, 2 cups meat mixture, 1 1/4 cups ricotta cheese mixture and 2/3 cup mozzarella cheese. Repeat layers. Top with the remaining noodles, meat mixture and the mozzarella cheese; sprinkle with Parmesan cheese.
4. Bake, covered, 30 minutes. Bake, uncovered, 10-15 minutes longer or until cheese is melted. Let the lasagna stand 10 minutes before serving.

Nutrition Info:

- Info392 cal., 12g fat (5g sat. fat), 89mg chol., 691mg sod., 39g carb. (13g sugars, 8g fiber), 32g pro.

Soups, Stews, And Chilis Recipes

Hearty Cabbage Soup

Servings:8
Cooking Time: 20 Minutes
Ingredients:

- 3 tablespoons canola oil
- 1 pound ground chicken
- 1 onion, chopped fine
- 2 teaspoons caraway seeds, toasted
- Salt and pepper
- 5 garlic cloves, minced
- 1 teaspoon minced fresh thyme or ¼ teaspoon dried
- ½ teaspoon hot smoked paprika
- ¼ cup dry white wine
- 1 head green cabbage (2 pounds), cored and cut into ¾-inch pieces
- 8 cups unsalted chicken broth
- 1 bay leaf
- 12 ounces red potatoes, unpeeled, cut into ¾-inch pieces
- ½ cup low-fat sour cream
- 1 tablespoons minced fresh dill

Directions:

1. Heat oil in Dutch oven over medium heat until shimmering. Add chicken, onion, caraway seeds, and ¼ teaspoon salt and cook, breaking up chicken with wooden spoon, until chicken is no longer pink and onion is softened, 7 to 9 minutes.
2. Stir in garlic, thyme, and paprika and cook until fragrant, about 30 seconds. Stir in wine, scraping up any browned bits, and cook until nearly evaporated. Stir in cabbage, broth, and bay leaf and bring to simmer. Reduce heat to medium-low, cover, and cook for 15 minutes. Stir in potatoes and continue to cook until vegetables are tender, 15 to 20 minutes.
3. Discard bay leaf. Stir a few tablespoons of hot broth into sour cream to temper, then stir sour cream mixture and ½ teaspoon salt into pot. Stir in dill and season with pepper to taste. Serve.

Nutrition Info:

- Info240 cal., 11g fat (2g sag. fat), 40mg chol, 430mg sod., 18g carb (7g sugars, 5g fiber), 17g pro.

Green Pepper Skillet Chili

Servings: 4
Cooking Time:25 Minutes
Ingredients:

- 1 pound 93% lean ground beef
- 1 large green bell pepper, chopped (about 1 1/2 cups total)
- 1 (14.5-ounce) can stewed no-added-salt tomatoes with liquid
- 1 (1.25-ounce) packet chili seasoning mix
- 3/4 cup water

Directions:

1. Place a large nonstick skillet over medium-high heat until hot. Coat the skillet with nonstick cooking spray, add the beef, and cook until no longer pink, stirring frequently. Set aside on a separate plate.
2. Recoat the skillet with nonstick cooking spray, add the peppers, and cook 5 minutes or until the edges begin to brown, stirring frequently.
3. Add the remaining ingredients to the skillet and bring to a boil. Reduce the heat, cover tightly, and simmer 15 minutes or until peppers are very tender, stirring occasionally, using the back of a spoon to crush the tomatoes while cooking.
4. Remove from the heat and let stand 10 minutes to develop flavors.

Nutrition Info:

- Info150 cal., 5g fat (1g sag. fat), 35mg chol, 390mg sod., 16g carb (7g sugars, 3g fiber), 13g pro.

Sausage & Greens Soup

Servings:6
Cooking Time: 20 Minutes
Ingredients:

- 1 tablespoon olive oil
- 2 Italian turkey sausage links (4 ounces each), casings removed
- 1 medium onion, chopped
- 1 celery rib, chopped
- 1 medium carrot, chopped
- 1 garlic clove, minced
- 6 ounces Swiss chard, stems removed, chopped (about 4 cups)
- 1 can (14 1/2 ounces) no-salt-added diced tomatoes, undrained
- 1 bay leaf
- 1 teaspoon rubbed sage
- 1 teaspoon Italian seasoning
- 1/2 teaspoon pepper
- 1 carton (32 ounces) reduced-sodium chicken broth
- 1 can (15 ounces) no-salt-added cannellini beans, rinsed and drained
- 1 tablespoon lemon juice

Directions:

1. In a 6-qt. stockpot, heat oil over medium-high heat. Add the next four ingredients; cook 6-8 minutes or until sausage is no longer pink and vegetables are tender. Add garlic; cook 1 minute.
2. Stir in Swiss chard, tomatoes, bay leaf and seasonings. Add broth; bring to a boil. Reduce heat; simmer, covered, 10-12 minutes or until Swiss chard is tender. Stir in beans and lemon juice; heat through. Remove bay leaf.

Nutrition Info:

- Info155 cal., 5g fat (1g sat. fat), 14mg chol., 658mg sod., 18g carb. (5g sugars, 5g fiber), 11g pro.

Classic Lentil Soup

Servings:6
Cooking Time: 45 Minutes
Ingredients:

- 1 tablespoon canola oil
- 2 slices bacon, chopped fine
- 3 garlic cloves, minced
- 1 teaspoon minced fresh thyme or ¼ teaspoon dried
- 1¼ cups French green lentils, picked over and rinsed
- 1 (14.5 ounce) can no-salt-added diced tomatoes, drained
- 1 onion, chopped fine
- 1 carrot, peeled and cut into ¼-inch pieces
- ¼ teaspoon salt
- ¼ teaspoon pepper
- 1 bay leaf
- ¾ cup dry white wine
- 4 cups unsalted chicken broth
- 1½ cups water
- Balsamic vinegar

Directions:

1. Heat oil in Dutch oven over medium heat until shimmering. Add bacon and cook until rendered and crisp, about 3 minutes. Stir in garlic and thyme and cook until fragrant, about 30 seconds.
2. Stir in lentils, tomatoes, onion, carrot, salt, pepper, and bay leaf and cook until vegetables are softened and lentils are darkened in color, 8 to 10 minutes.
3. Stir in wine, scraping up any browned bits, and cook until nearly evaporated, about 3 minutes. Stir in broth and water and bring to simmer. Reduce heat to medium-low, partially cover, and cook until lentils are tender but still hold their shape, 30 to 45 minutes.
4. Discard bay leaf. Stir in up to 1 tablespoon vinegar to taste. Serve.

Nutrition Info:

- Info250 cal., 7g fat (1g sag. fat), 5mg chol, 270mg sod., 30g carb (4g sugars, 8g fiber), 13g pro.

Quick Beef And Vegetable Soup

Servings:6
Cooking Time:18minutes
Ingredients:

- 1 pound 93 percent lean ground beef
- 2 carrots, peeled and cut into ½-inch pieces
- 1 onion, chopped
- 2 garlic cloves, minced
- 1 tablespoon no-salt-added tomato paste
- 2 teaspoons minced fresh thyme or ½ teaspoon dried
- Salt and pepper
- 4 cups low-sodium beef broth
- 2 cups water
- 1 (14.5-ounce) can no-salt-added diced tomatoes
- 8 ounces Yukon Gold potatoes, peeled and cut into ½-inch pieces
- 6 ounces green beans, trimmed and cut into 1-inch lengths
- 2 tablespoons chopped fresh parsley

Directions:

1. Cook beef, carrots, onion, garlic, tomato paste, thyme, ⅛ teaspoon salt, and ¼ teaspoon pepper in Dutch oven over medium-high heat, breaking up beef with wooden spoon, until beef is no longer pink, about 6 minutes. Stir in broth, water, tomatoes and their juice, and potatoes. Bring to simmer, then reduce heat to low, cover, and cook until potatoes are almost tender, about 10 minutes.

2. Stir in green beans and cook, uncovered, until vegetables are tender and soup has thickened slightly, 10 to 12 minutes. Stir in parsley and season with pepper to taste. Serve.

Nutrition Info:

- Info200 cal., 5g fat (2g sag. fat), 50mg chol, 470mg sod., 18g carb (5g sugars, 4g fiber), 19g pro.

Creamy Butternut Soup

Servings:10
Cooking Time: 20 Minutes
Ingredients:

- 1 medium butternut squash, peeled, seeded and cubed (about 6 cups)
- 3 medium potatoes (about 1 pound), peeled and cubed
- 1 large onion, diced
- 2 chicken bouillon cubes
- 2 garlic cloves, minced
- 5 cups water
- Sour cream and minced fresh chives, optional

Directions:

1. In a 6-qt. stockpot, combine first six ingredients; bring to a boil. Reduce heat; simmer, covered, until vegetables are tender, 15-20 minutes.

2. Puree soup using an immersion blender. Or, cool slightly and puree soup in batches in a blender; return to pan and heat through. If desired, serve with sour cream and chives.

Nutrition Info:

- Info112 cal., 0 fat (0 sat. fat), 0 chol., 231mg sod., 27g carb. (5g sugars, 4g fiber), 3g pro.

Garden Minestrone

Servings:8
Cooking Time:18minutes

Ingredients:

- 3 tablespoons extra-virgin olive oil
- 1½ pounds yellow summer squash, halved lengthwise, seeded, and cut into ½-inch pieces
- Salt and pepper
- 1 large onion, chopped fine
- 6 garlic cloves, minced
- 2 tablespoons no-salt-added tomato paste
- 2 teaspoons minced fresh thyme or ½ teaspoon dried
- ½ cup dry white wine
- 8 cups unsalted chicken broth
- 1½ pounds tomatoes, cored, seeded, and chopped coarse
- 2 (15-ounce) cans no-salt-added cannellini beans, rinsed
- 8 ounces green beans, trimmed and cut into 1-inch lengths
- 1 Parmesan cheese rind (optional), plus 1 ounce Parmesan, grated (½ cup)
- 1⅓ cups whole-wheat orzo
- 1 cup coarsely chopped fresh basil

Directions:

1. Heat 1 tablespoon oil in Dutch oven over medium heat until shimmering. Add squash and ¼ teaspoon salt, cover, and cook until squash has released its liquid, about 3 minutes. Uncover, increase heat to medium-high, and continue to cook, stirring occasionally, until squash is dry and lightly browned, about 3 minutes. Transfer squash to plate and wipe pot clean with paper towels.

2. Heat 1 tablespoon oil in now-empty pot over medium heat until shimmering. Add onion and ¼ teaspoon salt and cook until softened and lightly browned, 5 to 7 minutes. Stir in two-thirds of garlic, tomato paste, thyme, and ½ teaspoon pepper and cook until fragrant, about 1 minute. Stir in wine, scraping up any browned bits.

3. Stir in broth, tomatoes, cannellini beans, green beans, and Parmesan rind, if using. Bring to simmer and cook for 4 minutes. Stir in orzo, reduce heat to low, cover, and cook until green beans are just tender, 8 to 10 minutes.

4. Discard Parmesan rind, if using. Stir in squash and let sit until heated through, about 1 minute. Stir in basil, ⅛ teaspoon salt, remaining garlic, and remaining 1 tablespoon oil and season with pepper to taste. Sprinkle individual portions with grated Parmesan before serving.

Nutrition Info:

- Info300 cal., 8g fat (1g sag. fat), 5mg chol, 410mg sod., 42g carb (9g sugars, 10g fiber), 15g pro.

Fresh Corn & Potato Chowder

Servings:6
Cooking Time: 25 Minutes

Ingredients:

- 1 tablespoon butter
- 1 medium onion, chopped
- 1 pound red potatoes (about 3 medium), cubed
- 1 1/2 cups fresh or frozen corn (about 7 ounces)
- 3 cups reduced-sodium chicken broth
- 1 1/4 cups half-and-half cream, divided
- 2 green onions, thinly sliced
- 1/2 teaspoon salt
- 1/4 teaspoon freshly ground pepper
- 3 tablespoons all-purpose flour
- 1 tablespoon minced fresh parsley

Directions:

1. In a large saucepan, heat butter over medium-high heat. Add the onion; cook and stir 2-4 minutes or until tender. Add the potatoes, corn, broth, 1 cup cream, green onions, salt and pepper; bring to a boil. Reduce heat; simmer, covered, about 12-15 minutes or until potatoes are tender.

2. In a small bowl, mix the flour and remaining cream until smooth; stir into soup. Return to a boil, stirring soup constantly; cook and stir 1-2 minutes or until slightly thickened. Stir in parsley.

Nutrition Info:

- Info200 cal., 8g fat (5g sat. fat), 30mg chol., 534mg sod., 26g carb. (6g sugars, 3g fiber), 7g pro.

Coconut Curry Vegetable Soup

Servings:6
Cooking Time: 25 Minutes
Ingredients:

- 1 tablespoon canola oil
- 2 celery ribs, chopped
- 2 medium carrots, chopped
- 6 garlic cloves, minced
- 1 tablespoon minced fresh gingerroot
- 2 teaspoons curry powder
- 1/2 teaspoon ground turmeric
- 1 can (14 1/2 ounces) vegetable broth
- 1 can (13.66 ounces) light coconut milk
- 1 medium potato (about 8 ounces), peeled and chopped
- 1/2 teaspoon salt
- 1 package (8.8 ounces) ready-to-serve brown rice
- Lime wedges, optional

Directions:

1. In a large saucepan, heat oil over medium heat. Add celery and carrots; cook and stir 6-8 minutes or until tender. Add garlic, ginger, curry powder and turmeric; cook 1 minute longer.
2. Add broth, coconut milk, potato and salt; bring to a boil. Reduce heat; cook, uncovered, 10-15 minutes or until potato is tender. Meanwhile, heat rice according to package directions.
3. Stir rice into soup. If desired, serve with lime wedges.

Nutrition Info:

- Info186 cal., 8g fat (4g sat. fat), 0 chol., 502mg sod., 22g carb. (3g sugars, 2g fiber), 3g pro.

Italian Veggie Beef Soup

Servings:12
Cooking Time: 30 Minutes
Ingredients:

- 1 1/2 pounds lean ground beef (90% lean)
- 2 medium onions, chopped
- 4 cups chopped cabbage
- 1 package (16 ounces) frozen mixed vegetables
- 1 can (28 ounces) crushed tomatoes
- 1 bay leaf
- 3 teaspoons Italian seasoning
- 1 teaspoon salt
- 1/2 teaspoon pepper
- 2 cartons (32 ounces each) reduced-sodium beef broth

Directions:

1. In a 6-qt. stockpot, cook ground beef and onions over medium-high heat for 6-8 minutes or until the beef is no longer pink, breaking up the beef into crumbles; drain.
2. Add cabbage, mixed vegetables, tomatoes, seasonings and broth; bring to a boil. Reduce heat; simmer soup, uncovered, for10-15 minutes or until the cabbage is crisp-tender. Remove bay leaf.

Nutrition Info:

- Info159 cal., 5g fat (2g sat. fat), 38mg chol., 646mg sod., 14g carb. (6g sugars, 4g fiber), 15g pro.

Tilapia Stew With Green Peppers

Servings: 4
Cooking Time:40 Minutes
Ingredients:

- 1 medium green bell pepper, chopped
- 1 (14.5-ounce) can stewed tomatoes with Italian seasonings
- 1 cup water
- 1 pound tilapia filets, rinsed and cut into 1-inch pieces
- 1/2 teaspoon seafood seasoning

Directions:

1. Place a large saucepan over medium heat until hot. Coat the pan with nonstick cooking spray, add the bell pepper, and cook 5 minutes or until beginning to lightly brown, stirring frequently.
2. Add the tomatoes and water, increase to high heat, and bring to a boil. Reduce the heat, cover tightly, and simmer until the tomatoes are tender. Using the back of a spoon, break up the larger pieces of tomato.
3. Add the fish and seasonings and stir very gently. Increase the heat to high and bring just to a boil. Reduce the heat, cover tightly, and simmer 3 minutes or until the fish is opaque in the center. Remove from the heat and let stand, covered, 10 minutes to develop flavors.

Nutrition Info:

- Info150 cal., 2g fat (0g sag. fat), 55mg chol, 350mg sod., 10g carb (6g sugars, 2g fiber), 24g pro.

Golden Summer Peach Gazpacho

Servings:8
Cooking Time: 20 Minutes
Ingredients:

- 3 cups sliced peeled fresh or frozen peaches, thawed
- 3 medium yellow tomatoes, chopped
- 1 medium sweet yellow pepper, chopped
- 1 medium cucumber, peeled and chopped
- 1/2 cup chopped sweet onion
- 1 garlic clove, minced
- 1/3 cup lime juice
- 2 tablespoons rice vinegar
- 1 tablespoon marinade for chicken
- 1 teaspoon salt
- 1/4 teaspoon hot pepper sauce
- 1 to 3 teaspoons sugar, optional
- Chopped peaches, cucumber and tomatoes

Directions:

1. Place the first six ingredients in a food processor; process until blended. Add lime juice, vinegar, marinade for chicken, salt and pepper sauce; process until smooth. If desired, stir in sugar.
2. Refrigerate, covered, for at least 4 hours. Top individual servings with additional chopped peaches, cucumber and tomatoes.

Nutrition Info:

- Info56 cal., 0 fat (0 sat. fat), 0 chol., 342mg sod., 13g carb. (8g sugars, 2g fiber), 2g pro.

Creamy Potato Soup With Green Onions

Servings: 3
Cooking Time:15 Minutes
Ingredients:

- 2 cups fat-free milk
- 1 pound baking potatoes, peeled and diced
- 3 tablespoons no-trans-fat margarine (35% vegetable oil)
- 1/4 teaspoon salt
- 1/4 teaspoon black pepper
- 3 tablespoons finely chopped green onions, green and white parts

Directions:

1. Bring the milk just to a boil in a large saucepan over high heat (catch it before it comes to a full boil).
2. Add the potatoes and return just to a boil. Reduce the heat, cover tightly, and simmer 12 minutes or until the potatoes are tender.
3. Remove from the heat and add the margarine, salt, and pepper. Using a whisk or potato masher or handheld electric mixer, mash the mixture until thickened, but still lumpy.
4. Spoon into individual bowls and sprinkle each serving with 1 tablespoon onions.

Nutrition Info:

- Info200 cal., 5g fat (1g sag. fat), 5mg chol, 360mg sod., 32g carb (9g sugars, 2g fiber), 8g pro.

Creamy Chicken Rice Soup

Servings:4
Cooking Time: 30 Minutes
Ingredients:

- 1 tablespoon canola oil
- 1 medium carrot, chopped
- 1 celery rib, chopped
- 1/2 cup chopped onion
- 1/2 teaspoon minced garlic
- 1/3 cup uncooked long grain rice
- 3/4 teaspoon dried basil
- 1/4 teaspoon pepper
- 2 cans (14 1/2 ounces each) reduced-sodium chicken broth
- 3 tablespoons all-purpose flour
- 1 can (5 ounces) evaporated milk
- 2 cups cubed cooked chicken

Directions:

1. In a large saucepan, heat oil over medium-high heat; saute carrot, celery and onion until tender. Add garlic; cook and stir 1 minute. Stir in rice, seasonings and broth; bring to a boil. Reduce heat; simmer, covered, until rice is tender, about 15 minutes.
2. Mix flour and milk until smooth; stir into soup. Bring to a boil; cook and stir until thickened, about 2 minutes. Stir in chicken; heat through.

Nutrition Info:

- Info322 cal., 11g fat (3g sat. fat), 73mg chol., 630mg sod., 26g carb. (6g sugars, 1g fiber), 28g pro.

21-Day Meal Plan

Day 1
Breakfast: Open-faced Poached Egg Sandwiches
Lunch: Turkey & Apricot Wraps
Dinner: Grilled Swordfish With Eggplant, Tomato, And Chickpea Salad

Day 2
Breakfast: Blackberry Smoothies
Lunch: Weeknight Skillet Roast Chicken
Dinner: Cheese Manicotti

Day 3
Breakfast: Breakfast Grilled Swiss Cheese And Rye
Lunch: Chicken Strips Milano
Dinner: Hurried Hummus Wraps

Day 4
Breakfast: Stuffed Mushrooms
Lunch: Chicken Piccata
Dinner: Thai-style Red Curry With Cauliflower

Day 5
Breakfast: Yogurt Parfaits
Lunch: Asian Lettuce Wraps
Dinner: Garden Harvest Spaghetti Squash

Day 6
Breakfast: Roasted Vegetable Strata
Lunch: Mediterranean Chicken Pasta
Dinner: Stir-fried Tofu With Shiitakes And Green Beans

Day 7
Breakfast: English Muffin Melts
Lunch: Wild Rice Salad
Dinner: Broccoli And Toasted Nut Pilaf

Day 8
Breakfast: Steel-cut Oatmeal With Blueberries And Almonds
Lunch: Chicken Cucumber Boats
Dinner: Tasty Lentil Tacos

Day 9
Breakfast: Ginger-kale Smoothies
Lunch: Italian Spaghetti With Chicken & Roasted Vegetables
Dinner: Country Vegetable And Thyme Quiche

Day 10
Breakfast: Apple Spiced Tea
Lunch: Chicken Apple Sausage And Onion Smothered Grits
Dinner: Zucchini On Bleu Cheese Pasta

Day 11
Breakfast: Peach Cranberry Quick Bread
Lunch: Roasted Chicken Thighs With Peppers & Potatoes
Dinner: Stacked Vegetables & Ravioli

Day 12
Breakfast: Frittata With Spinach, Bell Pepper, And Basil
Lunch: Stovetop Tarragon Chicken
Dinner: Black Beans With Bell Peppers & Rice

Day 13
Breakfast: Cheesy Mushroom Omelet
Lunch: Apple-glazed Chicken Thighs
Dinner: Greek-style Garlic-lemon Potatoes

Day 14

Breakfast: Fried Eggs With Sweet Potatoes And Turkey Sausage
Lunch: Tuna & White Bean Lettuce Wraps
Dinner: Honey-buttered Acorn Squash

Day 15

Breakfast: Gorgonzola Polenta Bites
Lunch: Cajun Baked Catfish
Dinner: Confetti Corn

Day 16

Breakfast: Basil Spread And Water Crackers
Lunch: Nut-crusted Cod Fillets
Dinner: Slow-cooked Whole Carrots

Day 17

Breakfast: Tuna Salad Stuffed Eggs
Lunch: Garlic Tilapia With Spicy Kale
Dinner: Roasted Vegetables With Sage

Day 18

Breakfast: Tomato-jalapeno Granita
Lunch: Cheesy Shrimp And Grits
Dinner: Roasted Cauliflower

Day 19

Breakfast: Mango Avocado Spring Rolls
Lunch: Halibut En Cocotte With Cherry Tomatoes
Dinner: Squash & Mushroom Medley

Day 20

Breakfast: Asian Marinated Mushrooms
Lunch: Lime-cilantro Tilapia
Dinner: Roasted Smashed Potatoes

Day 21

Breakfast: Cheesy Tortilla Rounds
Lunch: Oven-roasted Salmon
Dinner: Mashed Cauliflower With Sour Cream

INDEX

Chicken Strips Milano 24
Classic Lentil Soup 87
Coconut Curry Vegetable Soup 90
Confetti Corn 45
Country Vegetable And Thyme Quiche 41
Couscous With Saffron, Raisins, And Toasted Almonds 55
Creamy Apricot Fruit Dip 18
Creamy Butternut Soup 88
Creamy Chicken Rice Soup 92
Creamy Chipotle Chile Sauce 36
Creamy Potato Soup With Green Onions 92
Creole-simmered Vegetables 47
Curried Chicken Meatball Wraps 20

D

Dark Chocolate Bark With Pepitas And Goji Berries 64

E

Easy Marinated Flank Steak 80
Egg Roll Noodle Bowl 78
English Muffin Melts 14

F

Farro Salad With Cucumber, Yogurt, And Mint 55
Fresh Corn & Potato Chowder 89
Fried Eggs With Sweet Potatoes And Turkey Sausage 17
Fried Green Tomato Stacks 83
Frittata With Spinach, Bell Pepper, And Basil 16
Fusilli With Zucchini, Tomatoes, And Pine Nuts 51

G

Garden Harvest Spaghetti Squash 38
Garden Minestrone 89
Garlic Tilapia With Spicy Kale 32
Garlicky Braised Kale 48
Ginger-kale Smoothies 15
Golden Summer Peach Gazpacho 91
Golden Zucchini 48
Gorgonzola Polenta Bites 18
Gran's Apple Cake 71
Grapefruit-zested Pork 83
Greek-style Garlic-lemon Potatoes 44
Green Bean & Potato Salad 76

Green Pepper Skillet Chili 86
Grilled Flank Steak With Summer Vegetables 84
Grilled Swordfish With Eggplant, Tomato, And Chickpea Salad 33

H

Halibut En Cocotte With Cherry Tomatoes 34
Hearty Cabbage Soup 86
Herb Garden Lasagnas 43
Herbed Chicken With Warm Bulgur Salad And Yogurt Sauce 61
Holiday Cookies 68
Homemade Guacamole 18
Honey-buttered Acorn Squash 44
Hurried Hummus Wraps 37

I

Italian Cabbage Soup 63
Italian Meatball And Escarole Soup 58
Italian Sausage & Provolone Skewers 25
Italian Spaghetti With Chicken & Roasted Vegetables 27
Italian Veggie Beef Soup 90

L

Lemon Vinaigrette 74
Lentil Pumpkin Soup 62
Lime-cilantro Tilapia 35

M

Mango Avocado Spring Rolls 22
Mashed Cauliflower With Sour Cream 47
Mediterranean Chicken Pasta 26
Mediterranean Chopped Salad 72
Mediterranean Tuna Salad 78
Mocha Pumpkin Seeds 21

N

Nectarines And Berries In Prosecco 66
No-fry Fish Fry 36
Noodles With Mustard Greens And Shiitake-ginger Sauce 49
North African–style Chickpea Salad 53
Nut-crusted Cod Fillets 32

O

Oatmeal Cookies With Chocolate And Goji Berries 65
One-pan Roasted Pork Chops And Vegetables With Parsley Vinaigrette 81
Open-faced Poached Egg Sandwiches 12
Orecchiette With Broccoli Rabe And Sausage 54
Oven-roasted Salmon 36

P

Parmesan Pork Chops With Spinach Salad 82
Parmesan Potato Bake 54
Parmesan-peppercorn Dressing 73
Peach Cranberry Quick Bread 16
Peanut Butter Snack Bars 67
Penne With Chicken And Pan-roasted Broccoli 56
Penne With Fresh Tomato Sauce, Spinach, And Feta 50
Pesto Quinoa Salad 75
Pickled Shrimp With Basil 21
Pineapple Breeze Torte 66
Pomegranate And Nut Chocolate Clusters 64
Pork With Tomato Caper Sauce 81
Power Lasagna 85

Q

Quick Beef And Vegetable Soup 88

R

Red Snapper With Fresh Tomato-basil Sauce 31
Red, White & Blue Potato Salad 74
Roasted Cauliflower 46
Roasted Chicken Thighs With Peppers & Potatoes 28
Roasted Plums With Dried Cherries And Almonds 70
Roasted Smashed Potatoes 47
Roasted Sweet Potatoes With Cinnamon 52
Roasted Vegetable Strata 14
Roasted Vegetables With Sage 46
Rosemary Rice With Fresh Spinach Greens 51

S

Sausage & Greens Soup 87
Seared Scallops With Orange-lime Dressing 30
Seaside Shrimp Salad 73
Shredded Beef Tacos With Cabbage-carrot Slaw 59
Simply Seared Beef Tenderloin 79

Slow-cooked Peach Salsa 62
Slow-cooked Whole Carrots 45
Spiced Basmati Rice With Cauliflower And Pomegranate 53
Spinach, Apple & Pecan Salad 77
Squash & Mushroom Medley 46
Stacked Vegetables & Ravioli 42
Steel-cut Oatmeal With Blueberries And Almonds 15
Stir-fried Tofu With Shiitakes And Green Beans 39
Stovetop Tarragon Chicken 29
Strawberry Pot Stickers 69
Stuffed Mushrooms 13
Summer Macaroni Salad 75
Summer Squash "spaghetti" With Roasted Cherry Tomato Sauce 42

T

Tartar Sauce 35
Tasty Lentil Tacos 40
Tender Green Pepper'd Top Round 84
Teriyaki Beef Stew 63
Thai-style Red Curry With Cauliflower 38
Tilapia Stew With Green Peppers 91
Tomato-jalapeno Granita 21
Tuna & White Bean Lettuce Wraps 30
Tuna Salad Stuffed Eggs 20
Turkey & Apricot Wraps 23
Turkey Chili 57
Turkey Stuffed Peppers 60

W

Warm Farro With Fennel And Parmesan 52
Watermelon & Spinach Salad 77
Weeknight Skillet Roast Chicken 23
Wheat Berry Salad With Roasted Red Pepper, Feta, And Arugula 50
Whole-wheat Blueberry Muffins 67
Wicked Deviled Eggs 19
Wild Rice Salad 26

Y

Yogurt Parfaits 14

Z

Zucchini On Bleu Cheese Pasta 41

Printed in Great Britain
by Amazon

26797745R00057